The Lighthouse

Dudley Witney

The Lighthouse

Foreword by Thomas H. Raddall

New York Graphic Society · Boston

International Standard Book Number: 0-8212-0670-2
Library of Congress Catalog Card Number: 75-9103

First published in Canada by McClelland and Stewart Ltd.

First United States edition

New York Graphic Society books are published by
Little, Brown and Company

This edition must not be sold in Canada

Printed in Canada

This book
is dedicated to
the lighthouse keepers
and their families
in memory of their
hospitality

Contents

Foreword

Poets of a bygone age used to talk of a seaman's dangers as "the perils of the deep," but seamen themselves were never so content as when they had deep water under them and not a speck of dry land within a hundred or a thousand miles. There were storms on the deep to be sure, but a mariner could usually cope with weather in all that sea room. What he hated and feared was a lack of room. The harsh irony of his profession was that as he drew near to his desired haven he also approached reefs, shoals, preposterous cliffs that jumped out of the mist or the dark, and all the other elements of damage and death that made a ragged outline where the sea ended and the land began. When, in his own term, he "made the land" he was happy if he made it in daylight and saw a cape, a mountain, or some other feature that he could recognize and pick out on his chart. Landfall was a very different matter if he made it in thick weather or at night. Where am I? Which way must I sail now to find my destination? And what hazards lie between here and there? With the cry of "Land ho!" anxieties fell upon him with a rush.

The Atlantic coast of North America naturally faces to the east, which in general is the mother of bad weather. However hard they blow, the westerly winds are usually good ones. Summer or winter they clear off the fog, the drizzle, the snow, or in lower latitudes the heat haze and mirage that often blind the sailor's view of the coast. The easterlies, which may blow from any point between north and south round by the east, are the ones that fling snow or fog or spume on the face of the coast like cream-pie on the face of a clown. And these are the gales that raise mighty waves and dash them on that long lee shore.

Joseph Conrad once remarked, "To see! To see! This is the craving of the sailor, as of the rest of blind humanity. I have heard a reserved silent man, with no nerves to speak of, after three days of hard running in thick weather, burst out passionately, 'I wish to God we could get sight of something!' "

The first seamen to get sight of something on the Atlantic face of North America were Leif Ericson and the other Norse adventurers who followed him there by way of Iceland and Greenland. Nowadays we marvel at their hardihood, sailing over those cold northern seas to a far coast that had a multitude of dangers, all unknown. About the year 1000 A.D. Leif's son Thorvald sailed to the new lands in his father's old ship, and somewhere on the coast of "Markland" (Land of Forest, which may have been Newfoundland or Nova Scotia) the ship struck a reef and cracked her keel.

Norse ships were light and small, and Thorvald was able to float his craft inshore to a headland, where his men felled a tree, hewed a new keel, and fitted it into place. They stuck up the old keel on the headland as a mark for other voyages and called the place Keel Ness. It was the first seamark erected by man on the coast of North America.

The Norse voyages ended with the life of their Greenland colony, an utter disappearance during a gap of centuries in history, a mystery to this day. The foundations of their houses and their church remain to be seen in Greenland, and Icelandic sagas recount a few of their voyages to lands far south and west of Cape Farewell.

Nearly five centuries after Leif Ericson, Columbus set out across the North Atlantic in much warmer latitudes, heading for India by the west. As his ships drew far to the west their crews became uneasy and almost mutinous. They doubted a round world and feared the appalling edge of a flat one. To make it worse, the steady wind in these latitudes was always at their backs, thrusting them day and night towards the abyss.

One night in October 1492, watching from the high poop-deck of his *Santa Maria,* Columbus saw the glimmer of a light in the distance ahead and called others to look. According to the ship's journal, "It was like a wax candle rising and falling once or twice. Few believed that it indicated land, but the Admiral was sure that land was close." So it was, an island in what became known as the West

Indies. It was not what he was looking for but in the long run India was no matter. Here in the Americas there would be richer nations and prouder cities in time to come.

The significant point to all of you who turn the pages of this book is that all we have, and all we are, in the Americas today began with a questing seaman and a light on the shore. As the Europeans spread along the American mainland their sea trade multiplied, and for safety and guidance there had to be more and better lights along the shore. They were of two kinds, the harbour lights that said "Come in" or "This way if you please," and the many others on rugged capes and reefs that flashed a blunt "Keep off!"

In one of my first voyages as a boy I remember coming on deck and a gruff old skipper saying, "There's Cape Race! Took a good look – you may never again see it this close." And there it was in the sunlight of a winter morning, a high knuckle of rock on the out-thrust fist of Newfoundland, for centuries the first sight of land on the long wet way from Europe to Canada, and the last point of departure for sailors dead-reckoning on the voyage east. There on the cliff stood the lighthouse which had saved countless people from blind disaster, and beside it the insignificant-looking wireless telegraph shack that picked up the SOS of a stricken *Titanic*. Like many others of its kind, the lighthouse on Cape Race said two things to the mariner, "Keep off!" and at the same time, "Now you know exactly where you are."

Modern science, advancing in all directions, has much improved the art of navigation. Today's sea officer, pushing buttons and twirling dials, can in theory make his way from shore to shore and port to port without a sight of sun, stars, or anything on the land itself. However, the intricacies of science are fallible like every other contrivance. The modern sailor's radar and other gadgets are subject to uncanny blind spots or silences, as if old Davy Jones had reached up from his locker and struck a malicious finger in the works. Consequently, the sailor has not thrown away his sextant, his compass, or his binoculars, and when he makes the land at night particularly, he wants to see a light that he can recognize and pinpoint on his chart. Science or none, the old adage is still true. Seeing is believing.

Change has come to the lighthouse, too. No longer must a keeper with his family and assistant live in stoic isolation at its foot, year in, year out. Increasingly nowadays it is unmanned, an automatic flashing apparatus held aloft by a steel lattice tower, and serviced at intervals by technicians making their rounds by land, sea, or air. On the Canadian coast the authorities are getting rid of obsolete wooden buildings in many cases by tearing or burning them down. So the old-fashioned lighthouse is a vanishing species, like the sailing ship for which it was first designed, and which it served for centuries.

In this book you can read the story of lighthouses from ancient times to the present day, and see how they were made and how they worked. Dudley Witney's magnificent photographs will take you to some of the new ones and many of the old ones still faithful in their service on the Atlantic coast from Labrador to Florida. There is a dignity and beauty about many of them, as you can see, and these pictures will remind you also of their utility, not only in time past, but now. Whether in small coasters or in leviathan tankers, the seaman still depends very much on these lights along the shore.

Thomas H. Raddall

The Lore of Lights

The lighthouse – any lighthouse, whether huddled on a hilltop or perched precariously on rocks miles offshore – is a monument to the evolution of tribal primitive to civilized man. As scattered tribes grew and merged to become city-states and empires, man began to cross the seas and later the oceans to trade – and sometimes to fight–with those of other lands. Civilization spread largely by sea, and rudimentary navigational aids were early imprints of commercial man.

At first, simple hilltop beacons guided mariners safely into strange ports or back home. And then, sometime in the thousand years before Christ, the first lighthouses appeared. Wherever they stood, lonely and weather-whipped, they testified that man had grown secure enough on land to set about conquering the sea.

Those early lighthouses were ineffective, even for the limited needs of the mariners of the time. In poor weather, when they were most needed, they often could not be seen at all. The value of more modern lighthouses, on the other hand, lies in the brightness and intensity that has

been achieved in the lights themselves. The technological leap that first made it possible for even a guttering candle to be seen from miles away as a shaft of light did not come until late in the eighteenth century. At that time, in one of those glorious paradoxes of history, the modern lighthouse system which now girdles the globe may have had its genesis in one of the most uncivilized and barbaric acts of all – cannibalism. For, as we shall see, it was an Englishman, William Hutchinson, who was himself shipwrecked and nearly killed and eaten by fellow survivors, who was to pioneer the new technology.

The first lighthouse of which we have detailed records dates back to 300 B.C. History is predictably vague, but evidence suggests that Egyptians began building a tower on Pharos, an island at the mouth of Alexandria Harbour, about that time. Pliny, in his *Natural History,* says it was built by Sostratus of Cnidus on the command of one of the ptolemies, or emperors, in 285 B.C. The cost was 800 talents, a sum which, according to the calculations of one English historian in the late nineteenth

Left: Cape Elizabeth at night.
Above: A nineteenth-century engraver's conception of the Pharos of Alexandria.

The Colossus of Rhodes (below), one of the Seven Wonders of the World, may have been also used as a lighthouse. Opposite page: The lighthouse at Corunna (left) in Spain and the tower at Genoa (right).

Mediterranean, by some advanced civilization whose existence has been obliterated by time. Other scholars suggest that the Colossus of Rhodes, the heroic statue of Apollo that is certainly a gargantuan work of art, was also constructed as a lighthouse.

Among the earlier lighthouses were probably towers built by Libyans and Cushites in Lower Egypt, their fires maintained by priests and their acolytes. Lesches, a Greek poet of 660 B.C., mentions a guiding light for mariners at Sigeum in the Troad, and other writers of ancient Greece suggest that there was also a lighthouse of sorts at the Hellespont. However, if such structures did exist, they had disappeared by the heyday of the Roman Empire. The great lighthouse at Alexandria harbour, on the other hand, was in operation for 1,000 years, and the structure survived for another 500 before being destroyed by an earthquake. Like the Colossus of Rhodes, built at about the same time, the Pharos of Alexandria was described as one of the Seven Wonders of the World.

From contemporary writings, we know the Romans built a light tower about a half century before the birth of Christ at Ostia, one of their major ports. It rose over a hundred feet into the air and was topped by a flaming beacon. But Ostia apart, historians and archaeologists have been able to identify the remains of more than thirty lighthouses throughout the provinces of the Roman Empire. There was a lighthouse at Corunna on the northwest coast of Spain known as the Tower of Hercules because local lore had it that Hercules himself built it. When Caligula visited France in 40 A.D., he ordered a fire tower built at the harbour of Boulogne "to aid sailors who ply these waters." Almost 800 years later it still stood, and Charlemagne ordered it back in service. In time, it came to be known as *Tour d'Ordre* to the French – and as "The Old Man of Bullen" to English sailors. It survived until July 29, 1964, when it collapsed in a heap of stone and dust. It might have endured until today but for the fact that the people of Boulogne had weakened it by stealing bits and pieces while constructing other buildings nearby. Roman buildings were singularly durable, a fact reflected in the name given a Roman light tower on the heights alongside Dover harbour in Britain. It came to be called "The Devil's Drop of Mortar" because of the hardness of its construction.

But the Roman Empire collapsed and Europe entered the Dark Ages. So far as it is known, there were no lighthouses built during that eclipse of civilization, when

century, would work out to $2,500,000 in today's currency. Ancient writings say that its height was "100 statures of man" – or about 500 feet – and that in the upper chambers were windows facing seaward. Fires, or perhaps torches, were lit in these windows, and Josephus reports that on a clear day the flame was visible at a distance of 300 stadia, or some thirty miles. The structure, which apparently took twenty years to build, was dedicated " for the safety of mariners."

There were almost certainly other, earlier, structures built as navigational aids. Some scholars have even suggested that the myth of Cyclops, the giant with a solitary eye dead-centre in his forehead, may have originated in the primitives' fear of lighthouses built, perhaps in the

the old empire fragmented into warring tribal factions once more.

By 1100 A.D., however, the nations of Europe had begun trading among themselves once more, and again lighthouses were built. The Italians, who were the first to re-emerge as seafaring traders, built a light tower at Meloria in 1157, and soon after built others at Venice and Tino and one near the Straits of Messina. They also built the light of Genoa, which may have influenced the course of history.

The Genoa light, built in 1161, endured into the fifteenth century when, in 1449, its keeper was one Antonio Colombo, uncle of Christopher Columbus. It was probably there, in the tower by the Mediterranean, that young Christopher's blood first stirred to the call of

the sea and the puzzles of navigation. Uncle Antonio, the lighthouse keeper, was the most likely to have fired the young man's passion, since everyone else in the family was in the weaving trade.

Through the Middle Ages, Turkey, France, Germany, the Scandinavian countries, and, of course, Britain, all built light towers of one kind or another, and navigation lights inside harbours became relatively common. The famous Trinity House, set up by Henry VIII to aid mariners in 1514, subsequently became the great name in light-house building and maintenance. Historians, however, say it was little concerned with building lighthouses as such until the nineteenth century and reserved most of its energies for providing lights at harbours and a pilot service to guide ships through the more perilous coastal

about building lighthouses that were at one and the same time designed as navigational aids for ships on passage and as warnings of natural hazards.

At the mouth of the River Gironde, where it runs into the Bay of Biscay, there is a litter of islands and rocks that even today is a hazard for shipping. One particularly perilous area is the island of Cordouan. It is said that Charlemagne himself recognized the dangers and built a chapel on the island for priests whose task was to sound trumpets as a warning to vessels. When Edward the Black Prince ruled Saxony in the fourteenth century, he built a tower on the island with a fire on top as an aid to mariners. In any event, there were two such buildings on the island when, in 1584, the legendary architect Louis de Foix was ordered by Henri III to build a light tower. His monstrously elaborate structure took twenty-seven years to build because the great swell of the Atlantic, building up across thousands of miles of open ocean, began washing the island away. But, in 1611, de Foix, who had originally thought he could finish the 197-foot tower in two years, lit his fire of oak for the first time.

History generally ignores this achievement of the French because the Eddystone lighthouse, another pioneering light built almost a century later by the British, has a far more colourful history. The Eddystone rocks, fourteen miles off the port of Plymouth in southern England, are a legendary sailors' graveyard. They are so exposed that even trying to build on them seemed insane in 1696, when one Henry Winstanley, described as "a gentleman of Essex," was given a contract by the British government to erect a lighthouse there. Some say the first wooden building, which first showed a light in 1698, was sixty feet high; others claim it was eighty. Whichever, the first structure wasn't high enough, because in storms the waves are so high that the spray rose above the lighthouse and put out the sixty great tallow candles, and the force of the pounding was so great that the structure weakened substantially in the first winter. The next year Winstanley built the tower forty feet higher – and re-lit the candles. Then in 1703, he took a crew out to do repairs. While he was there, a terrible storm swept the entire structure away, drowning everyone. Two nights later, the H.M.S *Winchelsea* was wrecked there, an instant reminder that if a lighthouse was needed anywhere, it was at Eddystone.

It was not, however, until 1706 that work began on the second Eddystone lighthouse. This tower was circular, ninety-two feet high and also built largely of wood.

approaches. Navigation lights were usually not solely for navigation, nor were the buildings in which they were displayed actually built as lighthouses. Lights might be displayed in the towers and steeples of castles and churches built near the sea or a harbour. Coastal fire towers were often designed primarily as an early warning system. In Britain, for instance, a chain of such towers was built so that in the event of invasion an alarm fire could be lit in a tower that was visible from the next tower along the coast or on a route to the nearest garrison town.

Almost all early lighthouses were harbour lights. Their light came from open fires of coal or wood, which could not be seen from far off even in the clearest, calmest weather, although they were primarily designed to serve as homing bacons. Not until the sixteenth and seventeenth centuries did the French and then the English set

The Eddystone lighthouse built by Henry Winstanley.

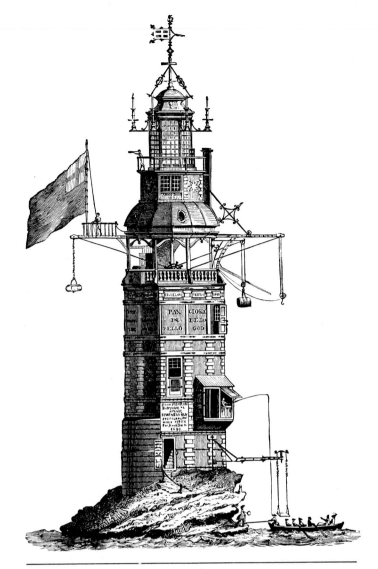

It was destroyed in 1755 by a fire that started in the candle room. The fire crept slowly down the tower, forcing the keepers from room to room until finally they stood on the rocks, watching helplessly. As one keeper, Henry Hall, gazed upward in awe and dismay, a glob of hot lead fell into his open mouth and ran down his gullet. Later, a doctor examined his mouth, could find no burns, and dismissed the story as imagination. When Hall died a few days later, an autopsy showed he had a half a pound of lead in his stomach.

The next Eddystone lighthouse was built by John Smeaton, who devised a technique for building wave-swept lighthouses which was to endure through the centuries. Smeaton's tower first showed a light in October 1759, and stood for over a hundred years until it was decided to build a higher structure 149 feet above sea level at low tide. That structure stands today.

The greatest expansion of trade from Europe to the Americas occurred during the sixteenth and seventeenth centuries. During this period, the number of lighthouses increased tremendously: D. Alan Stevenson, a British lighthouse historian, estimated that major lighthouses — that is, those that served as navigational aids and warning lights rather than as harbour lights — increased in number from thirty-four in 1600 to 175 in 1800.

The first lighthouse in the Americas was built at Vera Cruz, Mexico, late in the sixteenth century. The first North American lighthouse was Boston Light built on Little Brewster Island in 1716, and the second was completed by the French in 1733 at Louisbourg in Cape Breton, Nova Scotia. A 1728 map of Newfoundland mentions a lighthouse at Placentia, but since there is no other reference to it, and no relics to be seen, historians have concluded that the project was never begun.

Until the late 1700's, all the world's lighthouses had one thing in common: they were inefficient in bad weather or fog when they were most needed. Often, they were simply wood or coal fires set up on high land. The prevailing winds, which usually sweep in from the sea, blew the flames, and consequently most of the light, inland. Since many lighthouses with fires had no roofs (any enclosure soon filled with smoke, which made it impossible to keep the fire tended), rain often put the fires out. Tallow candles, usually weighing about a half-pound each, were often used. The third Eddystone had some thirty of these in a candelabra; the one in Boston is believed to have had about the same number. These candles provided little light, however, and were scarcely

more efficient than open fires. As late as 1801, celebrated hydrographer Francis Beaufort dismissed a proposal to put a lighthouse on Canada's notoriously dangerous Sable Island on the grounds that "nothing could be more mischievious than placing there a light . . . it could scarcely be seen further than the shoals extend and could therefore always act as an enticement into danger." Often the lighthouse light was hard to distinguish from, say, the lights of a house on a cliff. Indeed, in Britain, France, and along parts of the Canadian and New England coast, "wrecker" gangs would sometimes show a light actually designed to mislead navigators into thinking they were heading for a safe harbour, when, in fact, they were being enticed to rocks where their vessel would be wrecked and its cargo plundered. What was obviously needed was a way to magnify lights so that they were seen more clearly in bad weather, and distinguished more easily from other shore lights. It is here that William Hutchinson, the shipwrecked mariner, and cannibalism enter the story.

The first attempt to intensify a lighthouse beam was

made in 1727 by the French at the Cordouan tower. Mariners had complained they could not see the lighthouse more than a couple of miles out. In an attempt to increase the power of the light, a cone of wood was covered with tin plates and suspended, point down, above the fire. The reflection of the flames in the tin did make the light brighter, but the system was not adopted elsewhere, probably because soot from the fire constantly dulled the reflector and made the light difficult to sustain. In the 1730's, the Swedes also experimented with reflectors, but unsuccessfully. A better system was clearly needed, and it came in 1763 from William Hutchinson, who had the idea after what he later described as a "convivial evening" – the eighteenth-century euphemism for a night out with the boys.

At the time, Hutchinson was dockmaster of the port of Liverpool on Britain's northwest coast. He was committed to the improvement of navigation, and was responsible for building four lighthouses – harbour lights, rather – at Liverpool over the objections of the mayor and corporation of the city. They formally protested: "In regard those lighthouses will be no benefit to our Mariners, but a hurt, and expose them to more danger if trust to them; and also be a very great and unnecessary burden and charge to them." (From the start, lighthouses levied a tax on vessels using the port to pay maintenance costs and, in the case of privately owned lights, to make a profit.) It is a reasonable supposition that Hutchinson's early experiences as a sailor fired his enthusiasm for lighthouses. Although little is known of the man, the Historical Society of Lancashire and Cheshire (Liverpool harbour being partly in both counties) records that, "In early life he was shipwrecked, and the crew being without food they drew lots to ascertain who should be put to death to furnish a revolting and horrible meal to the survivors. The lot fell upon Hutchinson, but they were providentially saved by a ship which hove in sight. He afterwards observed this day as one of strict devotion."

But back to the convivial evening. It was apparently a gathering of "scientific gentlemen of Liverpool," one of whom wagered that he could read a newspaper by the light of a candle 200 feet away. He won by taking a wooden bowl, lining it with putty and sticking pieces of looking-glass, or mirror, into the putty. This contraption formed a reflector which, when the candle was placed in the centre, produced a sufficiently strong beam of light to illuminate the newspaper.

William Hutchinson borrowed the idea. Instead of a

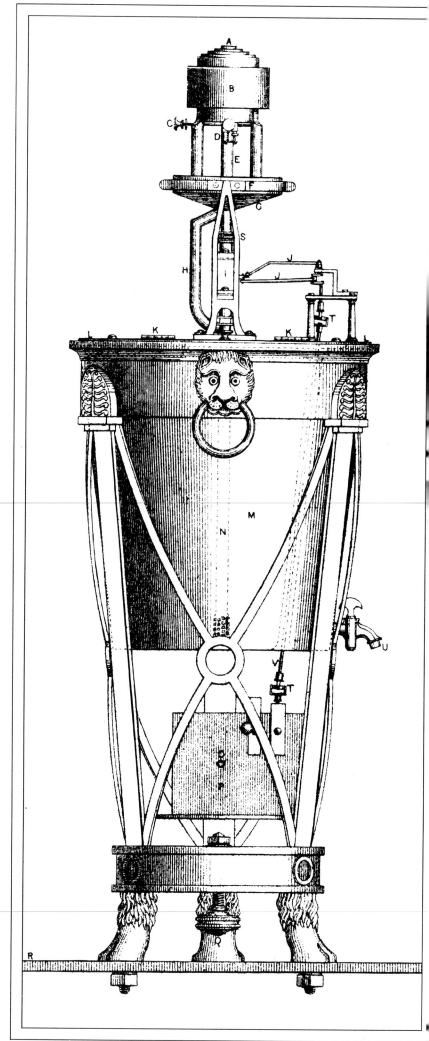

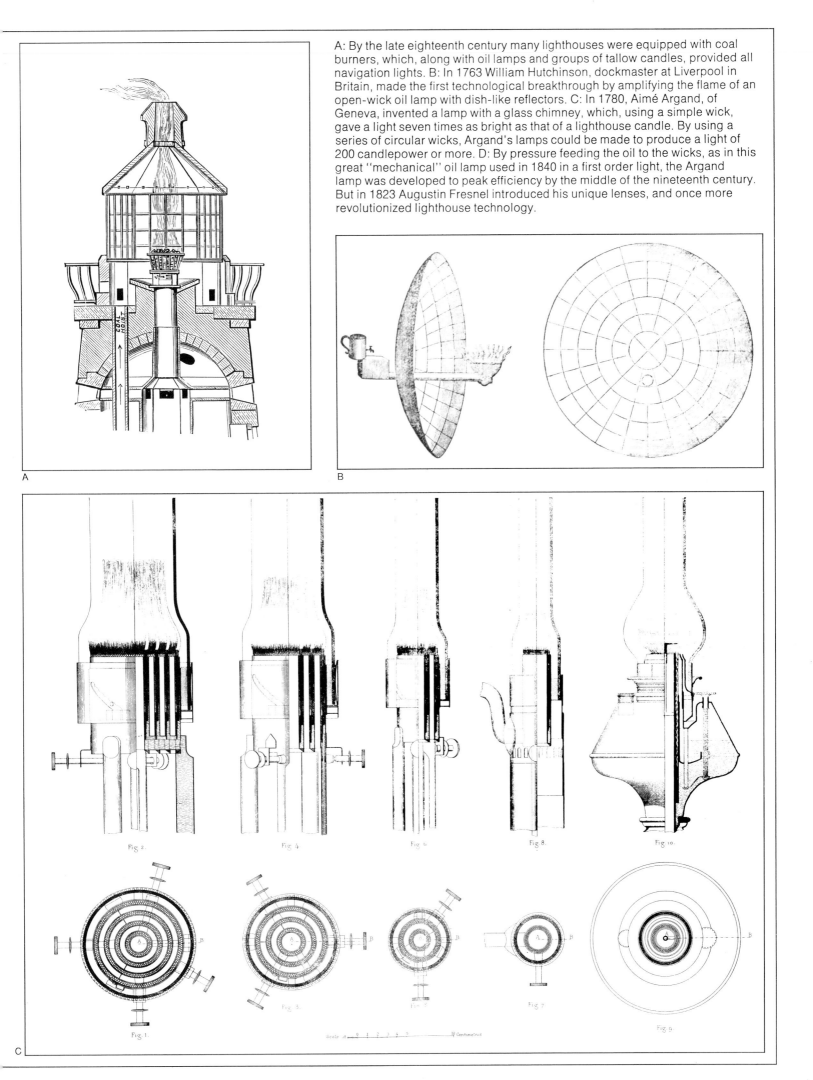

A: By the late eighteenth century many lighthouses were equipped with coal burners, which, along with oil lamps and groups of tallow candles, provided all navigation lights. B: In 1763 William Hutchinson, dockmaster at Liverpool in Britain, made the first technological breakthrough by amplifying the flame of an open-wick oil lamp with dish-like reflectors. C: In 1780, Aimé Argand, of Geneva, invented a lamp with a glass chimney, which, using a simple wick, gave a light seven times as bright as that of a lighthouse candle. By using a series of circular wicks, Argand's lamps could be made to produce a light of 200 candlepower or more. D: By pressure feeding the oil to the wicks, as in this great "mechanical" oil lamp used in 1840 in a first order light, the Argand lamp was developed to peak efficiency by the middle of the nineteenth century. But in 1823 Augustin Fresnel introduced his unique lenses, and once more revolutionized lighthouse technology.

A

B

C

Fig 2.   Fig 4.   Fig. 6.   Fig. 8.   Fig. 10.

Fig. 1.   Fig. 3.   Fig. 5.   Fig. 7.   Fig. 9.

Scale at 0 1 2 3 4 5 Centimetres

Below and right: The refinements of William Hutchinson's early reflectors gathered and focused most of the available light from an oil lamp into a beam. When used with early Fresnel lenses, the lights were four times more efficient. But since a beam of light can be readily seen only by vessels almost directly in its path, it was necessary to find a means of making the light sweep the horizon. The solution was groups of lights on a rotating table, and the principle of the modern apparatus at Charleston Lighthouse on Sullivans Island, South Carolina (bottom) differs from nineteenth century lights only in that it uses incandescent bulbs.

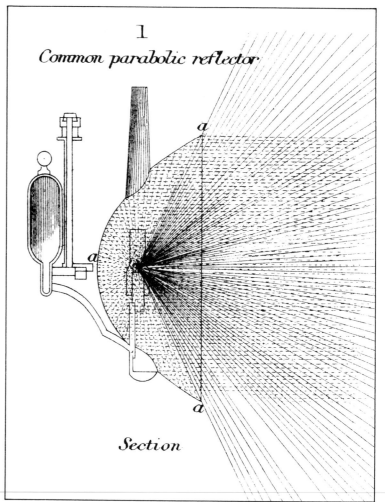

1

Common parabolic reflector

Section

When they adopted Fresnel lens lights in the late eighteenth century, the British shipped many of their reflector lights to the colonies. These were installed in east coast and Gulf of St. Lawrence lighthouses. The version at Cap d'Espoir in the Gulf (top), still an efficient navigation light, is unchanged except for the use of electric instead of oil lamps. The original apparatus at Bonavista Lighthouse, Newfoundland (above), was first used in Scotland. Bonavista is now a museum.

coal fire, the most common form of light, he decided on small oil lamps placed in the centre of a reflector. In his book *A Treatise on Practical Seamanship,* he wrote: "We have had and used here in Liverpool reflectors of 1, 2, and 3 feet focus and 3, 5½, 7½ and 12 feet in diameter. The smallest made of tin plates soldered together, and the largest of wood covered with plates of looking glass, and a copper lamp, the cistern part for the oil and wick stands behind the reflector to interrupt the blaze of the lamp acting upon it but the tube that goes through with a spreading burner mouthpiece to spread the blaze parallel thereto, and with the middle of it just in the focus or burning point of the reflector."

Thus the first really efficient lighthouse was born, although it was the French who perfected the idea in the early 1800's. In time, the reflectors were refined to a parabolic contour, a bowl-like shape that gathers rays from the available light into a concentrated beam. (A simple example of this principle today is the automobile headlight.) The arrangement came to be known as the catoptric system (from the Greek *katoptron,* or mirror), but was also known by English chauvinists as "The English System" as opposed to "The French System," which appeared in 1823. In that year, Augustin Fresnel introduced the dioptric system (from the Greek *dioptrikos,* to see through) which was the second and most significant breakthrough in lighthouse technology. Fresnel designed lenses that collected and focused the light rays into a horizontal beam far more efficiently than the reflector system. Fresnel's system and its adoption by the French government left the British behind. By mid-century, however, these systems had been combined, lamps using both reflectors *and* lenses were developed to provide the finest light of all.

A nineteenth-century experiment to compare the "French" and "English" systems, used as the measure the percentage of light from the lighthouse that actually reached an observer in a ship. It was found that only 3.5 per cent of the light from an open light of candles or fire reached the ship, while 17 per cent of the light from a reflector lamp reached it, and 83 per cent of the light from a Fresnel lens lamp could be seen.

Neither system would have been really effective but for the development in 1780 of the Argand burner, which became the first modern light source. Aimé Argand, who came from Geneva, discovered that an oil lamp with a cylindrical wick, confined within two concentric tubes and a glass chimney, produced a more brilliant light than any known up until that time. His efforts to perfect a new lamp had been in vain until the night his younger brother started messing with the equipment. The brother later gave this account: "My elder brother had long been trying to bring his lamp to bear. A broken-off neck of a flask was lying on the chimney piece; I happened to reach it over the table, and to place it over the circular flame of the lamp. Immediately it rose with brilliancy. My brother started from his seat in ecstasy, rushed upon me with a transport of joy and embraced me with rapture." The light produced by even an early Argand lamp with a one-inch wide wick was seven times as bright as that given off by a candle. By building lamps first with circular wicks and then with two or three wicks in concentric circles, Argand achieved fuller oxidation in the flame, thereby decreasing the smoke. The French found that a three-wick Argand lamp provided as much light as 200 candles. Another experimenter, American Benjamin Thomson, with papal title of Count Rumford, claimed that he had obtained from one simple Argand lamp twelve times as much light as from a candle.

Together, reflectors and the Argand lamp changed navigation. In 1763, Hutchinson's primitive oil lamp backed by reflectors could be seen from ten miles away, while the lamp alone would have been invisible at that distance. By 1819, scientific measurements were possible, and it was then reported that one silver-plated reflector, twenty-one inches in diameter, boosted the light of a seven-candlepower Argand lamp 350 times, to 2,450 candlepower.

Coal fires and candles were not entirely replaced until the mid-nineteenth century, and by then, lighthouses in Europe were mostly converted to oil. At about the same time, the United States adopted the Argand lamp. Sperm whale oil was largely used because it does not thicken in the cold. It soon became too expensive to use in Europe, but the U.S. whaling fleets kept American lights well and cheaply supplied. Other oils were tried, including olive oil. Reportedly, no oil was better than that used in the British lights at the Cape of Good Hope, where for a while they used oil made from the tips of the tails of local sheep, but they switched to rape seed oil when there were not enough sheep to keep up the supply.

From the middle of the nineteenth century, other light sources were tried. Lighthouses had coal gas mantles (and gas processing plants built alongside them to supply the gas), petroleum pressure lights, electric arc-lights, and, later, incandescent electric light bulbs.

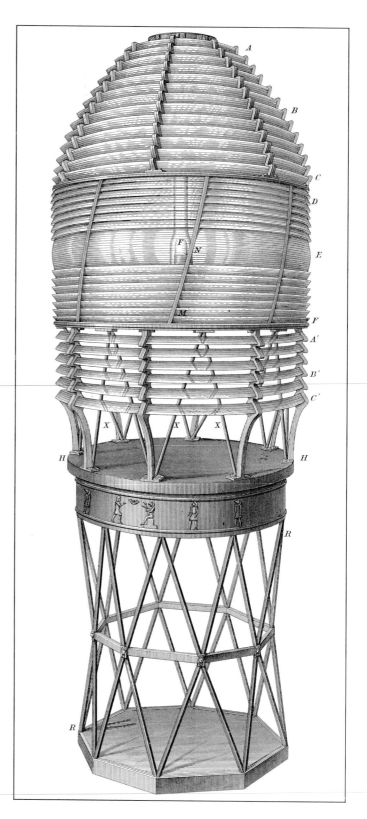

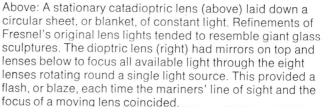

Above: A stationary catadioptric lens (above) laid down a circular sheet, or blanket, of constant light. Refinements of Fresnel's original lens lights tended to resemble giant glass sculptures. The dioptric lens (right) had mirrors on top and lenses below to focus all available light through the eight lenses rotating round a single light source. This provided a flash, or blaze, each time the mariners' line of sight and the focus of a moving lens coincided.

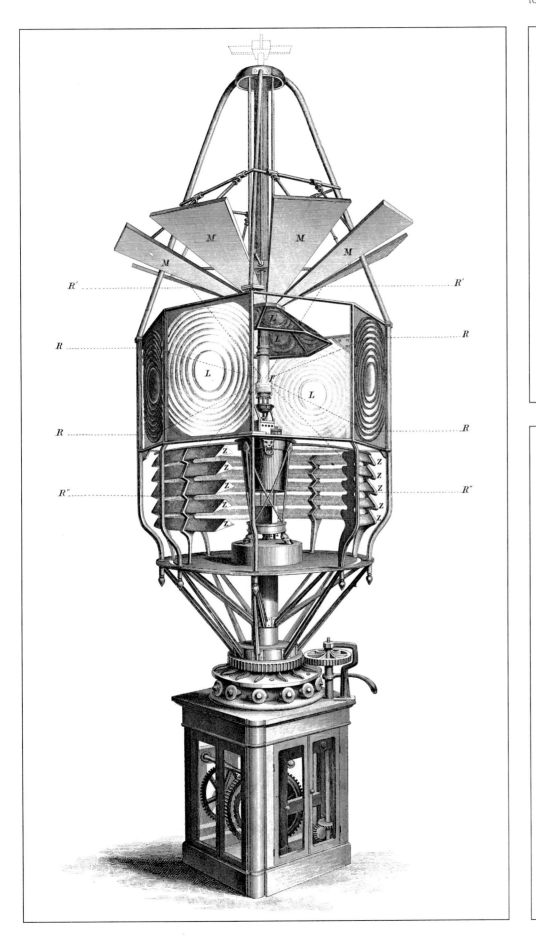

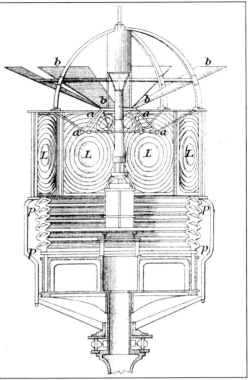

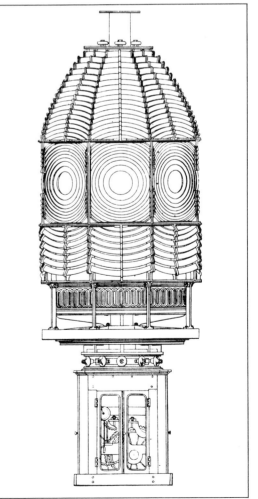

Throughout the world there are only a handful of the giant hyper-radial lenses. Typically, the one at Newfoundland's Cape Race lighthouse (previous page) has four lenses made from 6,720 pounds of glass, and the frames weigh another 4,800 pounds. The lenses alone are twelve-feet high and "float" in a bath of mercury. They are rotated by an electric motor the size of a shoebox. The entire installation weighs twenty tons and is so high it dwarfs its keepers (below).

Nevertheless, the Argand Lamp, or refinements of it, remained the most reliable source of light, particularly in the wave-washed lighthouses built at sea where neither gas nor electricity was readily available.

Great beams of light generated their own problems. A blazing fire or clutch of candles can be seen from all directions, but a focused beam of light cannot, except by those directly within its path. The need, therefore, was for a light to sweep the horizon so that it could be seen by all ships, whatever their position in relation to the lighthouse. The French first perfected a means of rotating either the light and reflectors or the lenses. This mechanism was a simple clockwork motor, similar to the works of a grandfather clock, with one descending weight activating the rotational movement.

As steamships supplemented and then supplanted sail, and as trade and shipping grew (particularly trans-Atlantic shipping carrying emigrants and goods to and from North America), there arose yet another problem — that of distinguishing one light from another. Two classic disasters are cited to demonstrate the perils of "fixed" lights that were hard to tell apart. One is the 1802 case of an East Indiaman that mistook the Hook light at Waterford in southern Ireland for the Eddystone in southern England, and was wrecked as a result. The other was the wreck of the 500-ton *La Jeune Emma* in November 1828. This ship had crossed the Atlantic from Martinique bound for Cherbourg. On sighting the Lundy light off the English coast, the captain mistook it for Ushant. Of nineteen people aboard, thirteen drowned, including a niece of the Empress Josephine.

It was not, however, until the latter part of the nineteenth century that techniques were developed for making lighthouse lights flash or "occulate," so that mariners could tell one from the other by the frequency and duration of the flashes. Oddly, although the British and Europeans at this time led the field in lighthouse technology, it was the North Americans who appear to have first met the need for a clear and positive means of distinguishing one light from another. It is reported that in 1798, a Cape Cod lighthouse was equipped with a screen revolving around the oil lamps so that their light would be obscured at intervals. As technology advanced, the means of "flashing" the lights became far simpler.

The use of kerosene was a major innovation in lighthouse illumination, but it was not introduced widely until twenty years after the fuel was discovered, or distilled, in 1846 by Dr. Abraham Gesner, a physician from Cornwallis, Nova Scotia. His "coal oil" was used in lighthouses in the St. Lawrence in the early 1860's, and its popularity grew in Canada because most lighthouses of the period still used the reflector lights and the bright flame produced by kerosene was more efficient.

When incandescent electric light bulbs began to be installed early in this century, the need for cumbersome mechanical equipment vanished, although Canada's lights were not totally converted to electricity until the 1940's. Electric lights of the arc-lamp variety were first tried in 1858 in Britain, but were not as reliable as oil

The first lighthouse in North America was built at Boston in 1716. It was destroyed during the War of Independence, and this detail of a 1729 engraving by William Burgis is one of the few illustrations of what that historic structure looked like. A new lighthouse was built after the American revolution, and that building is still in use.

lamps. Few lighthouses were ever permanently equipped with arc lamps.

But whatever the light source, reflectors and lenses made it possible for lighthousing to become a science, and four broadly international classifications of lights developed. There are landfall lights, major coastal lights, secondary coastal lights, and harbour lights, all using lighting apparatus of different size and intensity.

The development of lighthouses in Canada and the United States followed the same pattern as that in Europe. Thus, in the colonies also, the first lights were at important ports. Lights designed as navigational aids and to warn of hidden hazards—the light at Cape Hatteras warning of the treacherous shoal waters of the Outer Banks, for instance—came much later.

The first light in the North American colonies, the one at Boston, was a port light. In 1713, a group of local merchants petitioned the Massachusetts General Court asking for a "Light Hous and Lanthorn on some Head Land at the Entrance of the Harbor of Boston for the Direction of Ships and Vessels in the Night Time bound unto the said Harbor." Until this time, beacon fires had been lit by lookouts, but ships dependent on sail did not keep very strict schedules and would often turn up unexpectedly. The lighthouse, a lofty and graceful stone tower, was lit on September 14, 1716, its first keeper being one George Worthylake who was paid £50 a year by the General Court under the condition that if he neglected his duties he would be fined £100. America's first lighthouse keeper elected to follow the British system of lighting the light at sunset and extinguishing it at sunrise; this pattern opposed the Scottish lighthouse system

completed. The Americans won several battles on and for the island, but the British temporarily regained control and blew up the place in June 1776, when all the king's men finally sailed from Boston.

The British also destroyed North America's second lighthouse, the one built by the French at Louisbourg in Cape Breton. First lit in 1733, the light chamber caught fire – the light source was a simple sperm oil flame – and in 1736 had to be redesigned and replaced. In 1758, the British besieged and bombarded the great French fortress, and the lighthouse was damaged so badly that the victorious occupation forces decided it was not worth repairing.

As elsewhere, the real boom in lighthouse building did not hit North America until the nineteenth century. As steamships proliferated and trade boomed, lighthouses blossomed on headlands and offshore islands. Much of this activity was due to the success of the American Revolution. One of the first acts of the United States government was to set up a centrally administered lighthouse system for all thirteen states. Until the mid-nineteenth century, however, this system often functioned inefficiently. In 1852, Congress stepped in and revamped the system, appointing a lighthouse board consisting of two high-ranking naval officers, two army engineers, and a civilian scientist, plus a junior naval officer as secretary.

The state of the U.S. lighthouse system at this time can be measured by the fact that in 1850, by which time the major lighthouses of Europe were all displaying Fresnel's lens lights, almost all the U.S. lighthouses were equipped with the now outmoded reflector lights. Even so, the system had mushroomed at a staggering pace. In 1850, the U.S. lighthouses may have been inefficient, but there were an awful lot of them. At the end of the War of Independence there were just eleven lighthouses in the thirteen colonies. By 1800, there were sixteen. By 1852, there were 331 lighthouses and forty-two lightships. One of the first acts of the new board appointed in 1851 was to adopt the Fresnel lens light system. At the time of this decision, just three of those 331 lighthouses had lens lights. Five years later, 310 of them were so equipped.

By 1835, there were eleven lighthouses along the coasts of Nova Scotia, and the lighthouse commissioners of New Brunswick were claiming that the treacherous Bay of Fundy was so well lit that "an increase in lights would tend to perplex and embarrass the mariner on his voyage from seaward." Even so, by the late 1830's, it became apparent that Canada's coastal lighthouses were not

of showing the light only at dusk and extinguishing it at first light. The Scots saved money that way.

That first Boston light, supplemented by a cannon to serve as a fog signal in 1719, suffered from both the Puritan ethic and the American Revolution. Bostonians refused to erect a lightning rod on the tower, even though it was struck by lightning with fair regularity, on the grounds that it was "vanity and irreligion for the arm of flesh to avert the stroke of Heaven." It was, however, "the arm of flesh" that finally destroyed the lighthouse. In 1775, American revolutionary troops set fire to the tower to prevent its use by the British. The British set about repairing it, only to have George Washington send 300 men to invade the island and prevent the work from being very efficient. Until the beginning of the nineteenth century, most lighthouse construction in Canada was decided upon by commissions appointed specifically for that purpose. In 1805 the government of the Province of Canada set up its own lighthouse organization called the Quebec Trinity House. Next it established Montreal Trinity House to handle navigation on the upper reaches of the St. Lawrence.

In 1873, six years after Confederation, the federal Department of Marine and Fisheries took over both Trinity Houses, which by then administered a total of 110 lighthouses from the Strait of Belle Isle between Labrador and Newfoundland down to the upper reaches of the St. Lawrence, the Great Lakes, and the Pacific coast.

In both Canada and the United States, the lighthouse services had expanded massively by the turn of the century. Both countries introduced the last major reorganization at about the same time. In 1936, the Canadian Department of Marine was absorbed by the new Department of Transport, and in 1939 the U.S. lighthouse service became part of the Coast Guard. In the 1920's, the heyday of the lighthouses, both countries could boast first-class lighthouse systems – indeed, that of the United States was the largest in the world with a total of 16,888 aids to navigation, not all of them lighthouses, of course. Similarly, the total number on Canada's coasts and inland waterways about that time was 1,461, of which, records indicate, 105 were equipped with fog alarms – all part of the proliferation of bad-weather warning signals that took place during the nineteenth and early twentieth centuries.

Technology has changed, and navigational aids have improved with bewildering speed in the past century, but in essence the modern lighthouse remains a close cousin to its first known predecessor – the Pharos of Alexandria. Today's lighthouse has radar and fog signals, which are automatically turned on when sensors detect fog. There are also complex radio signals, and often a helicopter landing pad. Sometimes, the products of modern navigational technology seem endless. Many lights once proudly tended by men who grew old in the service are now automated, operated by transistorized equipment and self-contained computers. Soon, those lighthouses that remain may be operated by a central computer perhaps hundreds of miles away from the flashing light that is, when all the wonders of electronics fail, still the mariners' best friend. Even so, lighthouses are disappearing. New navigational techniques are rendering them obsolete. But there are some prophets who

see seamen becoming obsolete, too; there are predictions that ships will one day whiz across the oceans under the control of computers and be brought safely to harbour by a package of wires and transistors.

The lighthouses themselves will probably remain long after their lights have gone out and been replaced by other aids to navigation. The Pharos of Alexandria stood for 1,500 years before being demolished by an earthquake. Many of the lighthouses built in the past 300 years may well prove as durable. And if, as seems likely, they remain standing blindly atop a cliff or out at sea, they will still be what they were in the first place: monuments to the march of civilization and man's concern for his fellow creatures.

The great wave-washed lighthouses, like the one on Bell
Rock in Scotland, are among the most romantic buildings
ever erected. Designed by the legendary lighthouse builder
Robert Stevenson, the great tower was built on Bell (or
Inchcape) Rock. Begun in 1806, the 117-foot-high tower was
finished and the light lit on February 1, 1811.

Building the Towers

The Pharos of Alexandria, the first lighthouse of which we have an authenticated record, not only gave its name to the study and science of lighthouses (pharology), it also provided a model of splendour that has yet to be excelled. The island of Pharos stands at one of the yawning gaps in the North African coastline where the Nile spills out of the ages to muddy the impossible blue of the Mediterranean. It was partly because Pharos and the reef of which it was part provided a natural harbour that Alexander the Great decided to construct the great city of Alexandria nearby. The lighthouse itself was ordered by Ptolemy II, who decreed that a fire tower be built to help ships find their way past the shoals and into the harbour.

What was built was the most spectacular lighthouse ever seen before or since—presuming, that is, that stories about the Colossus of Rhodes being a lighthouse are untrue. Reference books tell us little about it, but in 1923 novelist E.M. Forster distilled his research on Alexandria in this description of the lighthouse:

It is not clear whether a divine madness seized the builders, whether they deliberately winged engineering with poetry and tried to add a wonder to the world. At all events they succeeded, and the arts combined with science to praise their triumph. Never, in the history of architecture has a secular building been thus worshipped and taken on a spiritual life of its own. It beaconed to the imagination, not only to ships, and long after its light was extinguished memories of it glowed in the minds of men. The lighthouse was made of local limestone, or marble, and of reddish-purple granite from Assouan. It stood in a colonnaded court that covered most of the promontory. There were four storeys. The bottom storey was over two hundred feet high, square, pierced with many windows. In it were the rooms (estimated at three hundred) where the mechanics and keepers were housed, and its mass was threaded by a spiral ascent, probably by a double spiral. There may have been hydraulic machinery in the central well for raising the fuel to the top; otherwise we must imagine a procession of donkeys who cease not night and day to circumambulate the spirals with loads of wood upon their backs. The storey ended in a cornice and in statues of Tritons: here too, in great letters of lead, was a Greek inscription mentioning the architect: "Sostratus of Cnidus, son of Dexiphanes, to the Saviour of Gods:

for sailors." The secondary storey was octagonal and entirely filled by the ascending spirals. The third storey was circular. Then came the lantern. The lantern is a puzzle, because a bonfire and delicate scientific instruments appear to have shared its narrow area.

Visitors speak, for instance, of a mysterious "mirror" up there, which was even more wonderful than the building itself. Why didn't this mirror crack, and what was it? A polished steel reflector for the fire at night or for heliography by day? Some writers describe it as made of finely wrought glass or transparent stone, and declare that when they sat under it they could

By the mid-1800's it was possible to build lighthouses on any hazardous rock, but not on equally dangerous sandy shoals. Then, in Britain, it was found that a light mounted on piles "screwed" into sand would withstand rough seas. In 1890 a tower (above) using this technique was built on Sand Key off the Florida coast. In the years since, the action of the sea has caused the island itself to disappear and reappear several times, but the tower still stands.

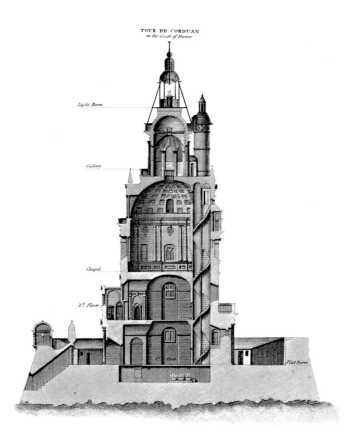

The spectacular Pharos of Alexandria has only been rivalled once – by the French in 1584, when they built a 197-foot-high structure (left) half palace and half lighthouse, on Cordouan at the mouth of the Gironde River. It took twenty-seven years to build and had an elaborate chapel on the second floor. Most of the present tower (right) on Cordouan Island is part of that original structure, but it was heightened by the addition of a plain brick tower in 1788.

see ships at sea that were invisible to the naked eye. Is it conceivable that the Alexandrian school of mathematics discovered the lens and that their discovery was lost and forgotten when the Pharos fell? Standing on the lantern, at a height of 500 feet above the ground, a statue of Poseidon struck the pious note. Other works of art are also reported: for example, a statue whose finger followed the diurnal course of the sun, a second statue who gave out with varying and melodious voices the various hours of the day, and a third who shouted an alarm as soon as a hostile flotilla set sail from any foreign port.

As if these splendours and mysteries weren't sufficient to make us wonder at what long-forgotten knowledge Pharos displayed, Josephus reports that its light could be seen at a distance of 300 stadia, or almost thirty nautical miles. It was to be 2,000 years before any other, newer lighthouse could make such a claim. Indeed, it was not until the French built the Cordouan light in the sixteenth century that any other lighthouse could remotely rival the splendours of the Pharos of Alexandria, or was, for that matter, designed solely as a navigational aid. Most of the lighthouses the Romans built were modelled on their first, the tower at Ostia, which has increasingly smaller storeys rising over 100 feet into the air. Although capped by a blazing fire, it was also a fortification to defend the port city.

The lighthouse that Caligula ordered built at Boulogne when he visited France in 40 A.D. was an octagonal shaft of red brick and grey and yellow stone that rose twelve storeys to 124 feet, each storey being slightly smaller than the one beneath it. The two towers built by the Romans at Dover on the English side of the channel bore a striking similarity to the one at Boulogne.

It was fitting, therefore, that it should be the Italians who built the most elaborate and durable towers when, after the Dark Ages, European nations began trading with one another. The British of the period contented themselves with church steeples and castle keeps. Typically, the tower of the little church that crowns St. Michael's in Cornwall, southwest England, had a stone lantern built on one side of it. The remains of the lantern, known as St. Michael's Chair, can still be seen. When, on the other hand, the Italians set out in 1544 to build a second tower at Genoa, they planned a structure 200 feet high that consisted of two towers, the smaller placed atop the larger. At that height the tower was prey to lightning, and in a bid to prevent its being struck the Genoans built a statue of St. Christopher nearby. It was less effective than the lightning rod they finally installed in 1778.

Since they for so long rivalled (and some say bettered) the English in lighthouse design and service, it is appropriate that it was the French who built the most ambitious lighthouse since the Pharos of Alexandria. This elaborate building was started in 1584 by Louis de Foix on the island of Cordouan at the mouth of the Gironde in the Bay of Biscay. For some obscure reason, however, the process of erosion seems to have speeded up almost as soon as he and his men began work. By the time they finished, twenty-seven years later, the island had been washed away. In fact, the lighthouse only survived because de Foix sunk a protective wave around the structure itself.

And what a structure. The lower section was 134 feet in diameter and contained the lighthouse keeper's apartments, plus a central hall, fifty-two feet in diameter. The second floor was a large chapel, and perched atop that – reaching a height of 197 feet – was a giant lantern and chimney designed for wood fires. Outside were pillars, parapets, ornate windows, statues, and frescoes. The spiral staircase was set off to one side so that the main part of the building would not be dirtied by attendants carrying wood to the fire.

The lighthouse of de Foix survives only in part today, as the building was partly rebuilt in 1788 when upper sections of the building were removed and replaced by a

Scale of   0 1 2 3 4 5   10   15   meters

The lighthouse at Cape Bonavista, Newfoundland, is no longer in use. However, the building is now a museum and the lights displayed there are a fine example of the British reflector-lamps developed in the late eighteenth and early nineteenth centuries. The monstrous clockwork (above) rotated the six reflector-lamps (right) which Robert Oke, a colonial lighthouse inspector of last century, said were originally installed in the great Bell Rock lighthouse in Scotland.

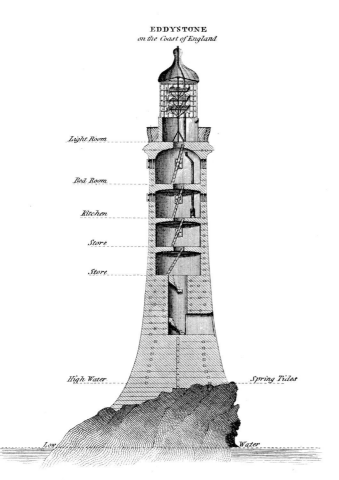

Light Room

Bed Room

Kitchen

Store

Store

High Water

Spring Tides

Low

Water

The third tower erected on the Eddystone rocks off the south coast of Britain was built by John Smeaton in 1756, and his technique of dovetailing the one-ton stones to those above and below became a model for the great wave-washed towers built around the world in later years. His tower might still be in use but for the fact that rocks on which it stood were undermined by the sea and a replacement structure had to be built in 1877.

---

circular stone tower 60 feet tall. Until early this century, the Cordouan lighthouse was considered the finest in the world, and some say it still is. Compared with other more modern lighthouses, the keeper's quarters are luxurious; at that time the French spared no expense to make the job of lighthouse-keeping an attractive one. At Frehel and at Stiff, about the same time, they built lighthouses with two towers joined by bridges on several floors. Keepers lived in one tower while tending the light in the other, thus avoiding soiling their quarters with coal dust and cinders from the fire.

Broadly speaking, all lighthouses can be divided into two categories – those on land, of which there are many types, and those perched on rocks at sea, called wave-washed lighthouses. The Cordouan light became perhaps the world's finest wave-washed light by chance, when the island eroded away around it. But it was finally the British who pioneered the great wave-washed lighthouses of drama and legend. Their first – the light on the Eddystone rocks fourteen miles at sea – was an ambitious undertaking. When Henry Winstanley announced he was going to build a lighthouse there in 1696 he was considered quite mad. Undeterred, he anchored his structure to the rocks with iron rods twelve feet long, enclosing the upper part of the rods in a circular stone base twelve feet high. The main polygonal structure was of wood, and elaborately encumbered with

galleries and gantries which offered considerable wind resistance. When within a year it was found that waves often put out the light, Winstanley went back, built an extension to the tower and added an outer ring of solid masonry which increased the diameter of the base from sixteen feet to twenty-four feet. In 1703 an epic storm blew up, swept the lighthouse off the rocks and drowned everyone, Winstanley included.

Three more towers were subsequently built at Eddystone, and in essence they alone demonstrate that the development of building methods for offshore wave-washed lighthouses are as valid today as they were when developed. Winstanley's wooden lighthouse was first replaced in 1706-9 when John Rudyerd built a ninety-two-foot-high circular tower, twenty-two feet eight inches at the base and fourteen feet three inches at the top, of simple design ideally suited to withstand wind and waves. It was, however, built partly of wood sheathing over stone so that when a fire started in the lightroom in 1755 it burned its way down the sheathing and the structure was a total loss. Next, in 1756, came John Smeaton's tower – perhaps the most famous of them all because it pioneered techniques that revolutionized lighthouse building and thus navigation as well. He, too, built a tapering circular tower – but of stone, each stone averaging about a ton and being dovetailed to the ones above and below. Smeaton's tower might have endured forever except that the rocks on which it stood were undermined by the sea. The present lighthouse was started in 1877; and as a result of a further refinement of Smeaton's building technique, it has remained the model for structures of its kind. That refinement was a solid, circular vertical base. Instead of tapering upwards from sea level, as did Smeaton's light and all others built prior to 1870, the new Eddystone light offered vertical circular walls to the pounding waves. This surface, it was found, broke up the waves, whereas the old tapering walls did not. In fact, the big problem was that the waves, hitting an inclined surface, simply ran up the walls. In heavy storms, water could reach even the highest lightrooms unless there was a gallery or cornice built beneath them to dam the water.

No refinements – and there were many – can diminish the significance of Smeaton's achievement in building the first lighthouse of dovetailed stone, however. His Eddystone tower was inspected by architects and engineers from all over Europe and North America, and its success made possible many similar lighthouses in

When built at the start of the 1800's, the 2,076-ton Bell Rock light, twelve miles off the coast of Forfarshire in Scotland, was considered one of the engineering wonders of the world. High spring tides submerge to a depth of sixteen feet the sandstone rocks on which it is built.

---

places where it had previously been thought impossible to place a light, however great the hazards to shipping. What Smeaton had done was to use building principles for what came to be called "monolithic lighthouses," principles that were later enshrined into the engineering dicta that (a) the centre of gravity should be as low as possible; (b) the mass of the structure must be such that it is in itself of sufficient strength to withstand wind and waves; and (c) the foundation should be deeply buried in solid rock. The application of these and other such engineering laws allowed for the construction of the 100-foot high Bell Rock light – a structure of 2,076 tons.

The Bell Rock lighthouse, twelve miles off the coast of Forfarshire in Scotland, is a classic example of an adaptation of Smeaton's principle to another circumstance. Built by the great lighthouse engineer Robert Stevenson, it stands on sandstone rocks which, during high tides, are submerged to a depth of sixteen feet.

Another famous adaptation is that used in building Minots Ledge lighthouse off Boston Harbour. Completed in 1860, the lower forty feet of the eighty-nine-foot tower is solid, and the rocks are keyed together vertically but not horizontally. Instead, the layers are tied together with bonding bolts. The Minots Ledge light was, in fact, the second to be built on the outermost of the Cohasset Rocks about twenty miles southeast of Boston, and it demonstrated the advantages of Smeaton-style solid rock lighthouses in exposed areas. Between 1832 and 1841, forty ships were wrecked on the rocks, and in 1847 it was decided to put a light there. Construction was started the same year, and the beacon was lit on January 1, 1850. The first structure was of openwork style based on nine iron piles, or legs, each sunk five feet into the rock. Engineering knowledge at the time insisted that such a structure would be secure, but the first two lighthouse keepers – one an old sea captain – promptly quit on the grounds that the structure was unsafe in storms. The third chief keeper was visiting the mainland in April 1851, when a particularly violent storm swept the lighthouse into the sea, killing the two assistant keepers on duty. Thus the first U.S. lighthouse that was exposed to the full force of the mighty Atlantic lasted barely a year. On the other hand, the Smeaton-style tower built to replace it still stands today.

Since wave-washed lighthouses were often built on rocks covered at high tide by the swirling ocean, caissons (walled-in chambers sunk into the seabed from which the seawater is pumped) had to be built in order for

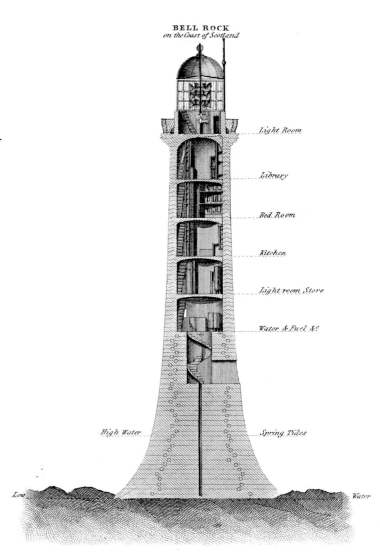

BELL ROCK
on the Coast of Scotland

Light Room

Library

Bed Room

Kitchen

Light room, Store

Water & Fuel &c

High Water   *Spring Tides*

Low   *Water*

workmen to put the foundations below sea level.

It wasn't until 1838, however, that a secure wave-washed lighthouse was built on soft ground. At that time a lighthouse was needed on the underwater shoal on Britain's east coast known as the Maplin Sands, which, as the name implies, hardly provide a suitable foundation for any structure. Besides needing a stable base, a structure built in the sea must be able to withstand the force of ocean currents and waves. For example, off the Atlantic shores of Britain, the average pressure of waves in winter is an astounding 2,068 pounds *per square foot,* with a maximum of 6,083 pounds per square foot pressure being recorded. When they were building the Dhu Heartach light, fourteen miles off the Island of Mull, Scotland, fourteen stones, each weighing two tons and set in cement thirty-seven feet above sea level, were washed away by waves. In 1860, at the famous Bishop Rock lighthouse – perhaps the most exposed in the world, receiving the full force of the Atlantic – storm waves tore loose the great fog-warning bell that weighed three hundredweight and was a hundred feet above sea level. So – how do you build a lighthouse on the Maplin Sands, where the sea, if not as thunderous as the Atlantic, is still a mighty force?

Experiments with screw pile foundations for lighthouses were first conducted on the Maplin Sands at the mouth of the River Thames, and the first such structure to come into use was the seven-legged light at Port Fleetwood in northern England (below). Using different principles, U.S. engineers built several pile lighthouses on the Florida reefs in the late 1800's. Alligator Reef light (top, opposite page) was completed in 1873.

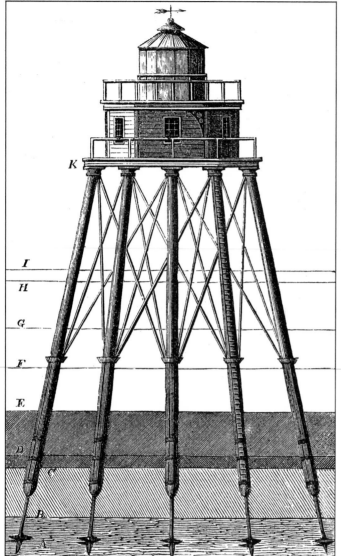

The problem was solved by designing a screw pile — that is, creating a shaft of iron, six inches in diameter with a single turn of the flange of a screw four feet in diameter at one end. And then you screw the pile twenty-two feet down into the stand, at which depth it will support up to sixty-four tons. Nine such piles support 576 tons — more than the weight of a capsule providing quarters for the keepers, plus the light itself. Although the methods of sinking the piles varied, the result of building lighthouses on them was a stable structure of openwork steel that offers far less resistance to hurricane force winds and waves than do solid stone lighthouses. One of the finest examples of this kind of construction is the 135-foot-high tower on the Alligator Reef in Florida. Not dissimilar is the American Shoal lighthouse, also in Florida, which was built in 1880 and is generally typical of the lighthouses that now line the Florida coast.

Caissons were also used for construction of lighthouses on sand and shoals. For example, the lighthouse at Fourteen Foot Bank in Delaware Bay was anchored to the sea floor using the caisson technique to construct a solid base on a shoal that lay twenty feet beneath the surface at low tide. In 1883, Major David P. Heap of the Lighthouse Board proposed to sink a cast iron cylinder thirty-five feet in diameter and seventy-three feet in

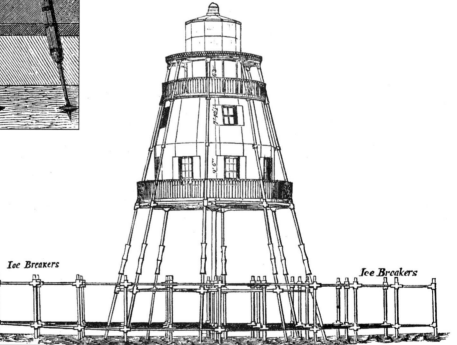

The first screw pile lighthouse in the United States was built in 1848 on Brandywine Shoal in Delaware Bay. Twenty years earlier, engineers had built an ordinary, non-screw pile structure there, but it was "demolished by the action of the sea" within twelve months. The replacement screw pile light (above) had a fence to prevent damage by floating ice in winter.

height on a square wooden caisson for the foundation of a lighthouse. Once properly moored and sunk to the bottom, the caisson was pumped dry. In the compressed air inside the caisson, three gangs of men worked around the clock with candles in their hats until they had excavated the sand to a depth of thirty-three feet. As they dug, the caisson and the concrete-filled cylinder descended into the sea floor to form a stable base for the lighthouse, which was later reinforced by a thousand tons of rip-rap placed at the base of the cylinder. Despite all this, later storms caused the lighthouse to tremble, and an additional 2,000 tons of rip-rap were needed to stabilize it.

Most U.S. lighthouses, however, were more solid in appearance. These costly and durable structures were usually built of brick or stone, or both. The first North American lighthouse, the one built in 1715-16 on Little Brewster Island in Boston Harbour, was similar to many of the shore lights erected in Europe through the eighteenth and nineteenth centuries. Some lighthouses were extraordinarily elaborate – like the Fort Thompkins lighthouse in New York built about 1900. Of wood, it was elaborately panelled and porticoed and was described by one scornful critic as "a fine example of institutional gingerbread."

The kind of light needed – whether a landfall light of

Holes were mined in uneven or sandy seabeds when building caisson lighthouses. The perils of building the Fourteen Foot Bank caisson light (below) in Delaware Bay are obvious from this engineers' drawing (below left) illustrating techniques used in laying the lighthouse foundation. The job, which actually cost $50,000 less than estimated, was completed in 1886.

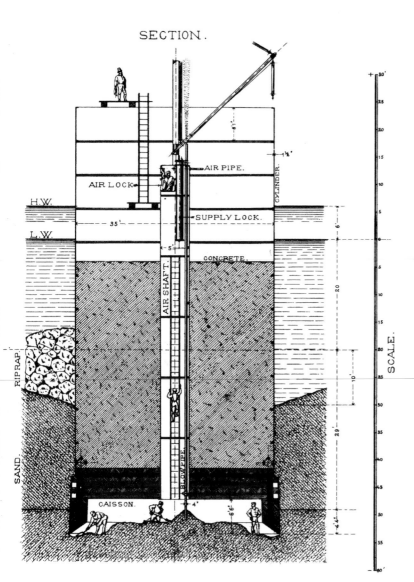

SECTION.

so-called first order, or a secondary coastal light – had a great effect on the design and location of the structure itself. Most of the great wave-washed lighthouses are both hazard and landfall lights, but there are many landfall lights on hand, mostly perched on clifftops. If the cliff is high enough, the structure can be relatively simple – just a modest tower, with the keeper's quarters located in an adjoining house. Many early lighthouses along the New England coast are arranged on this simple plan, but their appearance is no indication of their importance to mariners. Rather, it is the intensity of the light itself that matters to those at sea.

When all navigational light sources were fires and candles, no international agreement about determining a light's importance by its intensity was possible. But through the mid-nineteenth century, as the reflector and lens lights were adopted, standardization became possible, if only because there were only two or three manufacturers, first in France and later one in Britain. These firms produced a specific range of lights and, in so doing, more or less arbitrarily defined lighthouses for all time. A first order light of the kind that was installed at the great lighthouse of Navesink, New Jersey, remains one of the most beautiful objects in the world, something akin

The design and construction of Pemaquid Point light at the entrance to John's Bay, Maine, is typical of dozens of lighthouses built in New England immediately after the American Revolution. The towers were usually conical with walls of rubble stone masonry generally three feet thick at the base tapering to two feet at the top. Most were isolated and had sturdy frame houses attached.

The original wooden lighthouse built on Gannet Rock in the Bay of Fundy is still in use after almost 150 years.

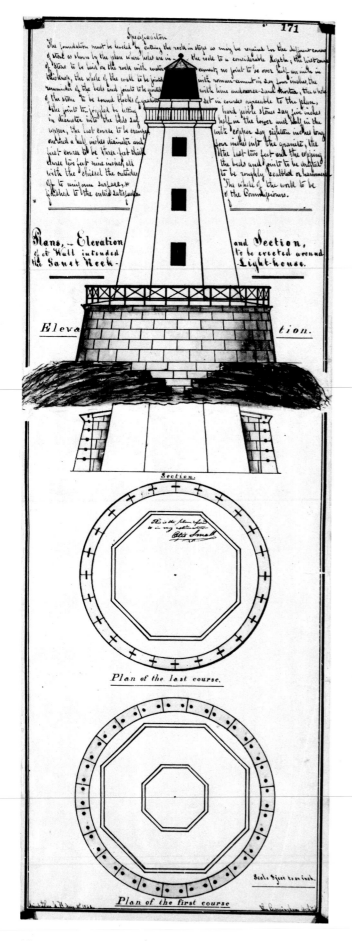

to that marriage of science and art that novelist E.M. Forster described in reference to the Pharos of Alexandria. As early as 1860, the British firm of Messrs. Chance, Brothers and Co., one of two great European manufacturers, defined a first order light apparatus as being twelve feet high, six feet in diameter, consisting of elaborate lenticular apparatus and an exquisitely complex yet singularly reliable lamp.

Since then, the Fresnel lens lights have been changed. Now they are generally made in seven sizes, or orders:

Order	Inside Diameter	Height
First	72⁷⁄₁₆″	7′10″
Second	55⅛″	6′1″
Third	39⅜″	4′8″
Three-and-a-half	29½″	3′8″
Fourth	19¹¹⁄₁₆″	2′4″
Fifth	14¾″	1′8″
Sixth	11¾″	1′5″

Generally, the fourth, fifth, and sixth "orders" of light are channel navigation lights, while lights of the third order are either major harbour or minor coastal lights.

Until the appearance of the hyper-radial lens, first order lights had the greatest glamour. Lighthouse engineer Alan Stevenson once wrote: "Nothing can be more beautiful than an entire apparatus for a fixed light of the first order. It consists of a central belt of refractors, forming a hollow cylinder six feet in diameter and thirty inches high; below it are six triangular rings of glass, ranged in a cylindrical form and above a crown of thirteen rings of glass, forming by their union a hollow cage composed of polished glass ten feet high and six feet in diameter. I know of no work of art more beautifully creditable to the boldness, ardor, intelligence and zeal of the artist."

The lighthouse at Navesink, New Jersey, produced light of twenty-five million candlepower even in 1898. And the original Eddystone had sixty candles!

First order lights are now generally so bright than the only limit to their range is the curvature of the earth; if they are too low they cannot be seen at a distance, and if they are too high they cannot be seen close up. Such lights are rarely higher than 200 feet, and most are lower.

While the United States built durable masonry lighthouses, early colonial Canada made do with wooden buildings, partly because they were cheaper and partly because wood was readily available. Canada's first two lighthouses – at Louisbourg and on Sambro Island – were masonry, but from then on, wood and later circular towers of iron plates were preferred in many cases. A surprising number of these wooden lighthouses still stand, among them the Gannet Rock light built in 1831 on a rocky island seven miles off the southern tip of Grand Manan Island, where it has been totally exposed to the elements for almost 150 years. The official description of the Cape Jourimain lighthouse at Cape Tormentine, New Brunswick, a building completed in 1870, would fit many lighthouses built in the mid- and late nineteenth century. It is an eight-sided tower of timber and frame, fifty feet high, with each of the eight sides tapering from twenty feet at the base to nine feet at the top. The ground level and first storey joists were thirteen inches by four inches, and the sides, floor, and hatchway of the lightroom were sheeted in galvanized iron as a fire protection. The tower was covered with high quality shingles. Not only was the construction typical, so was the shape.

The skeletal towers of openwork steel that first appeared elsewhere in the world in the mid-nineteenth century and were built up and down the U.S. coast are rarely seen in Canada. Far more common in Canada are the cylindrical towers of cast iron plates, which were pre-fabricated on land and hauled to the chosen site. The first of these to be erected in Canada was built at Cape Pine in Newfoundland in 1851. By 1906 these towers were appearing elsewhere in Canada – the first homemade ones being erected at Cape Norman in the Strait of Belle Isle and at Cape Bauld on the nearby northern coast of Newfoundland. Near the tower, a simple yet pleasant house was usually built for the keeper and his family. There they lived comfortably and usually in great isolation. Indeed, this description of a lighthouse keeper's life would apply up and down the coast of Canada and the United States until well into this century, when automated equipment became so reliable that permanent keepers could be dispensed with; and by being perpetually peripatetic, one or two technicians could, with periodic inspections, maintain many lights along a given stretch of coastline.

It has also been a long time since one of the great wave-washed lighthouses, like the Eddystone or the one at Minots Ledge, has been needed. Modern lighthouses are mostly of openwork structural steel construction or, like the ice-cheating, "wasp waisted" Prince Shoal light in the St. Lawrence, of concrete largely pre-cast in the comfort of a city cement plant and later towed out and sunk in place. They are wondrous places, these new structures, with accommodation for computers and radar housings and electronic signalling equipment and helicopter decks.

But for splendour and romance none can equal the ancient Pharos of Alexandria.

Minots Ledge Light

In North America, Minots light is the classic wave-washed lighthouse, a great pillar perched on rocks far out at sea as a symbol of man challenging the supremacy of the awesome North Atlantic. But while the present structure has triumphed over the ocean for more than a hundred years, the first lighthouse built there was defeated very quickly. It is said, even today, that the victims of that defeat still haunt the new structure.

Minots Ledge is one of the Quonahassit Rocks, a legendary graveyard off the mouth of Boston harbour. As shipping boomed during the mid-nineteenth century, the annual toll increased to the point that in the nine years prior to 1841 more than forty vessels foundered on Minots Ledge and nearby rocks. In 1847 the Treasury Department, then in charge of lighthouse construction, approved plans to build a lighthouse on iron piles sunk into the highest point of the ledge, a stretch of twenty-five-foot-wide rock exposed only at low tide on the calmest day. The seventy-five-foot-high lighthouse was first lit on January 1, 1850. On April 17, 1851, in a storm that was to become a legend, the lighthouse was swept off the rock, and the two assistant keepers drowned.

In 1855, the newly established Lighthouse Board, set up in response to complaints about the Treasury officers' inefficiencies, decided to replace it with a great stone tower modelled on those built on the Eddystone rocks off the shores of southern England. The task took five years. First, the ledge itself had to be levelled to accommodate the seven great granite blocks that would provide the foundations. The size of these can be guessed from the fact that in the second course, or layer, of granite blocks there were twenty-nine stones, each weighing about two tons.

The structure was completed in 1860, and almost immediately was said to be haunted by the ghosts of the two men who had drowned when the first lighthouse was washed away. Two lighthouse keepers reported that the lamp and lens had been brightly polished – but not by any flesh-and-blood keeper. Sailors passing the lighthouse insist they have heard strange voices and seen figures clinging to lower sections of the ladder. Some say that the ghost of one of the two dead keepers, a Portuguese, has been seen just prior to the predictably violent northeast storms, allegedly clinging to the lighthouse ladder calling out: "Keep away . . . keep away." In the first lighthouse, the keepers signalled to one another by tapping the stovepipe that ran up through the structure. There was no stovepipe in the stone lighthouse, but the two keepers reported hearing tapping.

In fairness to the builders of the original steel pile lighthouse, it must be said that such structures have survived throughout the world; it is just that they're not suitable for Minots Ledge. Some of the highest waves ever recorded have crashed against Minots light, the most terrifying reportedly being a wave that momentarily submerged the 100-feet-high tower. It still happens, but now there's no one there to record the fact: Minots Ledge became an automatic beacon in 1947. Its signal, however, is still a sequence of one-four-three flashes of light spaced over thirty seconds. That signal was decided upon in 1894, and ever since local lovers have claimed that it spells out the words: I love you.

Building Minots Ledge lighthouse, the first great wave-washed tower in North America, was a spectacular engineering achievement. The stones were cut and notched together on shore, as seen in this picture (top left). Then the tower was dismantled and shipped stone by stone to the offshore rock above. Sectional drawings (right) show the immense strength of the tower. The great granite blocks were dovetailed into one another at the sides, and each layer, or course, was anchored to those above and beneath by massive steel pins. The technique, which closely follows that pioneered in Britain, was necessary because of the force of the North Atlantic seas. Some of the biggest waves regularly smash across Minots Ledge .

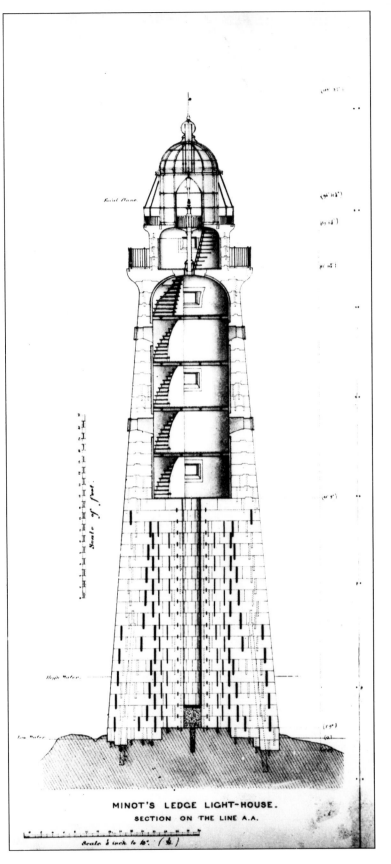

MINOT'S LEDGE LIGHT-HOUSE.
SECTION ON THE LINE A.A.

Scale ⅛ inch to 1ft. (⅛)

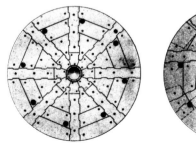

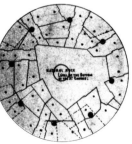

Above: Minots Ledge, Mass.

Opposite page
Top left: Detail of Fresnel lens, Tybee Light, Ga.
Top right: Lantern of Seguin Light, Me.
Lower left: Detail of modern lamp and reflector, Cape Lookout, N.C.
Lower right: First order lens, Sombrero Key Light, Fla.

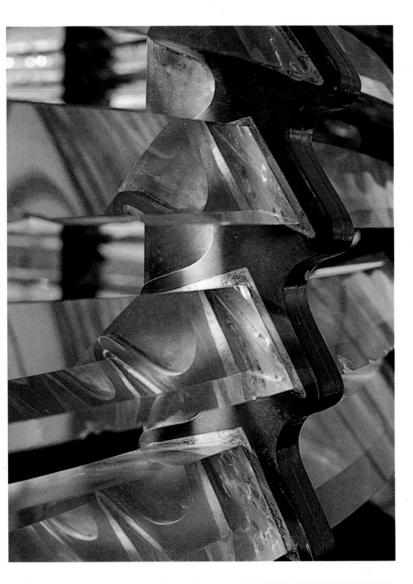

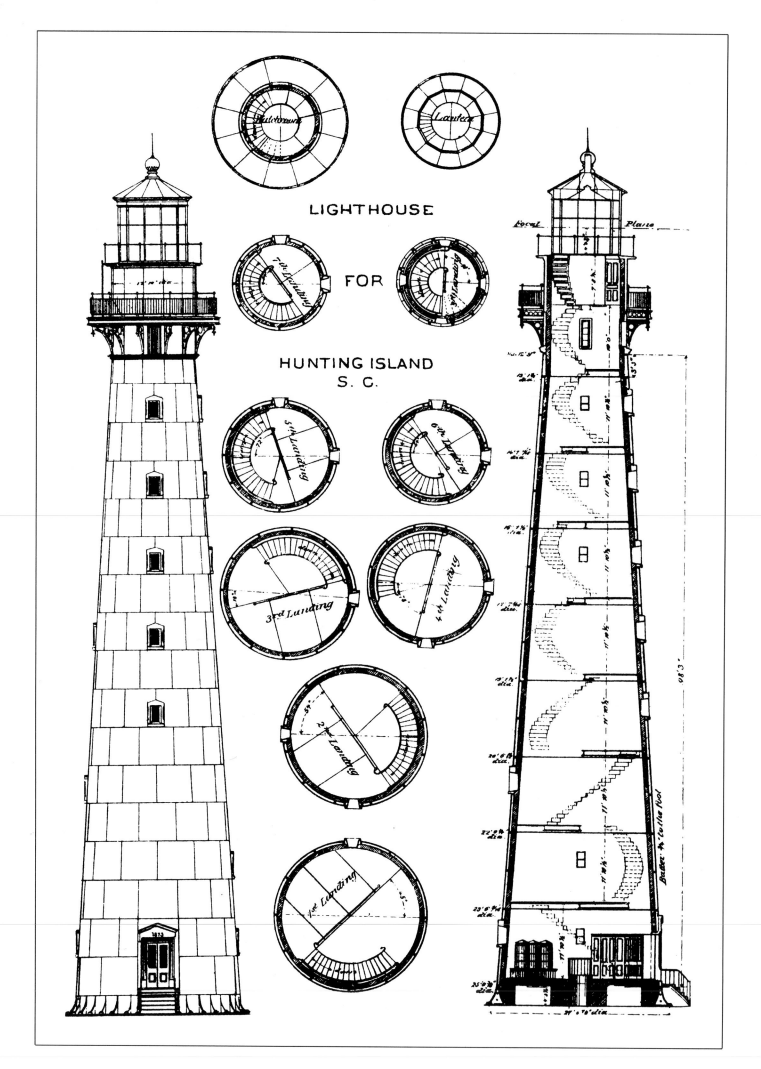

LIGHTHOUSE

FOR

HUNTING ISLAND
S. C.

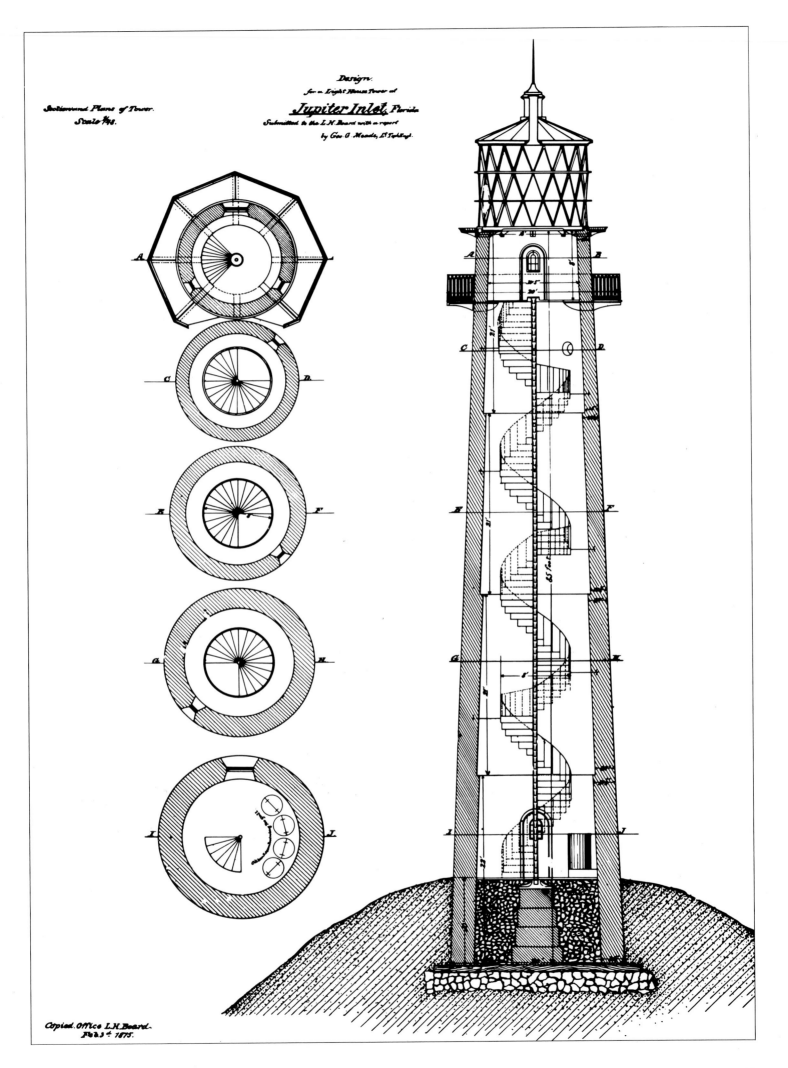

Sectional and Plans of Tower.
Scale ⅛".

Design.
for a Light House Tower at
Jupiter Inlet, Florida
Submitted to the L.H. Board with a report
by Geo. G. Meade, Lt. Topl. Engr.

Copied. Office L.H. Board.
Feb. 3rd 1875.

A   Father Point, Que.
B   Goose Rocks, Me.
C   Fame Point, Que.
D   New London Range, P.E.I.
E   Rockland Breakwater, Me.
F   Haszard Point Range, P.E.I.
G   Buzzards Bay Entrance, Mass.
H   Cape Henry, Va.

A

B

C

D

E

F

G

H

Scale.

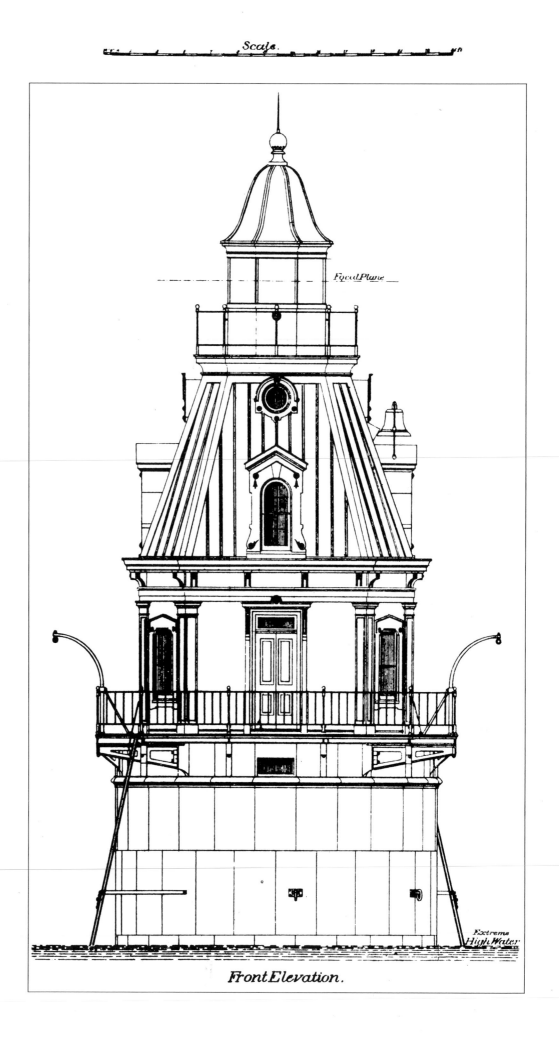

Fixed Plane

Extreme High Water

Front Elevation.

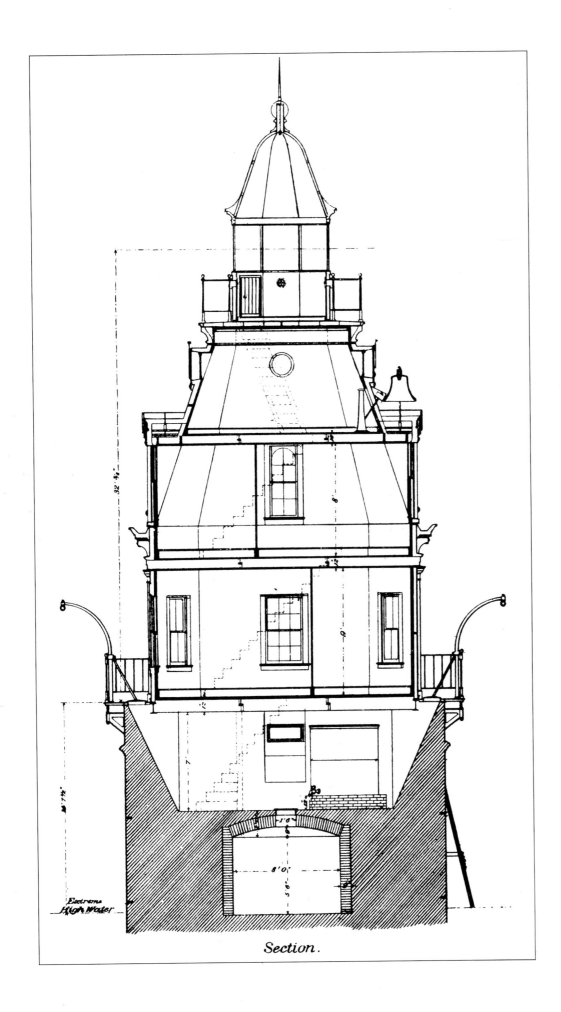

Section.

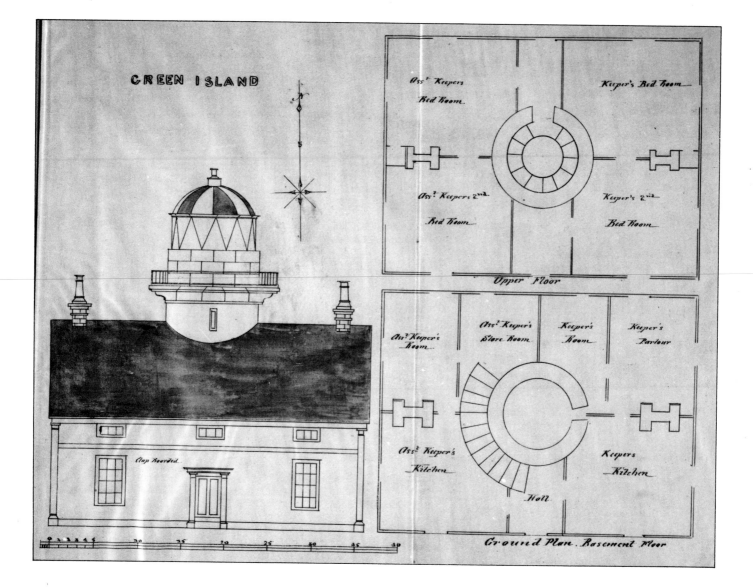

GREEN ISLAND

Ass.ᵗ Keepers Bed Room

Keeper's Bed Room

Ass.ᵗ Keepers 2.ⁿᵈ Bed Room

Keeper's 2.ⁿᵈ Bed Room

Upper Floor

Clap Boarded

Ass.ᵗ Keeper's Room

Ass.ᵗ Keeper's Store Room

Keeper's Room

Keeper's Parlour

Ass.ᵗ Keeper's Kitchen

Keepers Kitchen

Hall

Ground Plan. Basement Floor

Labrador Sea

Belle Isle, North End
Belle Isle, South End (Upper and Lower)

LABRADOR

QUEBEC

Pointe
Amour

Greenly
Island

Gull Island
(Cape Saint John)

Long Point (Twillingate)

CANADA

Cape Bonavista

Baccalieu Is.
(S.W. Point)

Pointe des Monts

St. Lawrence
River

Cap de la Madeleine

Cap Chat

Fame Point

ILE ANTICOSTI

Rivière à la Martre

Cap des Rosiers

Father Point

Prince Shoal Pier

Gulf of St. Lawrence

Bird Rocks

Lobster Cove Head

Corner Brook

NEWFOUNDLAND

Rose Blanche Point

Fort
Amherst
Cape
Spear

St. John's

Ferryland
Head
Cape
Race

MAGDALEN ISLANDS

Grindstone

Entry Island

St. Paul Island,
North Point and South Point

ST. PIERRE ET
MIQUELON (FRANCE)

Cape St. Mary's

NEW BRUNSWICK

MAINE

UNITED
STATES

PRINCE EDWARD ISLAND

New London
Range

Indian Head

Charlottetown

Cape North

East Point

Kidston Island (Baddeck)

Sydney

Wood Is.
Harbour
Range

Louisbourg

CAPE BRETON ISLAND

Tête de Galantry

Cape Pine

Moncton

Blockhouse Point

Saint John

Head Harbour
(Campobello Is.)

Bay of Fundy

Margaretsville

Halifax

NOVA SCOTIA

White Head Island

Maugher Beach

Country Island

Atlantic Ocean

SABLE ISLAND

Sable Island

Gannet Rock

Sambro

Swallowtail
(Grand Manan)

Yarmouth

Cape Fourchu

Seal Island

J.M.Master

55

Newfoundland

The coastline of Newfoundland – a tough granite strip of jagged rocks, so indented that if pulled into a straight line it would circle the globe – shelters thousands of small coves. It is on these rocks and in these coves that the saga of romance, adventure, loneliness, and danger that are the daily bread of the land's hardy people is written. Newfoundlanders are people with a deep sense of history.

Lying in the mouth of the Gulf of St. Lawrence, straddled by the Atlantic trade routes, Newfoundland's maritime life has had an influence far greater on history than has the island itself. For many, it was the beginning of the New World; for others, it has promised the riches of cod for food or great sperm whales for oil to light the lamps of Europe.

The sea has given plentifully, but it has also taken its toll. In the deep, grey, everlasting fogs that blanket the coasts and shipping lanes around them, and out in the shoals and sandbars which high seas hide from frail fishing boats, countless men have lost their lives. In the early nineteenth century, the records of the port of Bristol, in southwest England, show that an average of one in eight ships that sailed to the New World, never reached its destination. Prior to that, the losses were higher. Not all were wrecked off the coast of Newfoundland, but it was here that the toll was seemingly the highest. Two world wars added to this toll, and even today, the Strait of Belle Isle on the northern coast and the long rocky eastern coastline are nightmare areas for skippers.

The problem is geographic. Ships crossing the North Atlantic have a choice. They can head for the St. Lawrence River through the Strait of Belle Isle, a region only fifteen miles wide and about eighty miles long. Half the year it is iced in and impossible, and during most of the other half, it is fog-bound. Moreover, it is a hiding place for icebergs, and its northern shore is the rock-bound coast of Labrador. The other choice for ships making for Canada's mainland ports is to go south of the island of Newfoundland, a treacherous route that adds an extra couple of hundred miles to the journey. Steep, granite cliffs, which rise from deep on the ocean floor and edge a thousand inlets, lie to the north of this shipping lane, where fogs are notoriously thick and long-lasting.

The route south around Newfoundland through the Cabot Strait to the St. Lawrence is the entry to Canada most used by mariners. The rocks off Cape Race (seen here from the top of Cape Race lighthouse) are the greatest hazard on a generally perilous shoreline, and ships are warned to take frequent soundings when approaching the great landfall lighthouse that was the first sight of Canada for millions of immigrants.

Here lighthouses arrived late on the scene of shipping development. The first light on the island was at Fort Amherst, near St. John's harbour in 1813. It was not for another twenty years that other lighthouses were built around Newfoundland's coast, although lighthouses were not uncommon down the eastern seaboard of the United States a century prior to that. In the meantime, immigrants coming to Canada and to the United States were in dire peril. Thousands of lives were lost at sea in the great immigration period of the early nineteenth century. The unlit, barren islands off the shores of Newfoundland were strewn with wrecks. There, with the ship's back broken and the hulk washed off shore, the passengers awaited rescue by lighting fires and praying. Some lasted up to ten weeks before starvation drew them to a painful death. Others kept alive through cannibalism but were found in the spring by the fishing fleets as "petrified people caught by death in the act of doing nothing in particular."

Despite its dangers, the sea has always drawn men to it. The history of Newfoundland was shaped by rugged men and women. The first known settlers from outside the island left their marks on the east coast, near a port called L'Anse aux Meadows. Here the remains of tenth and eleventh-century Viking dwellings were recently unearthed. It appears these people came on a voyage which ended farther west, but that some stayed on the island. To these hardy men it must have been a paradise, for although the Newfoundland shores are uninviting to ships, and the offshore fogs are the worst in the world, these characteristics do not extend to the atmosphere and scenery inland.

The ancestors of today's Newfoundlanders were fishermen who had the courage to stay on the island when the fishing fleets returned home in the fall during the period when the British banned colonization, recognizing Newfoundland only as a temporary shelter for the cod fishing fleets. The discovery of the teeming shoals of cod made millionaires of many of these captains in the sixteenth century and gave Europeans a new winter diet.

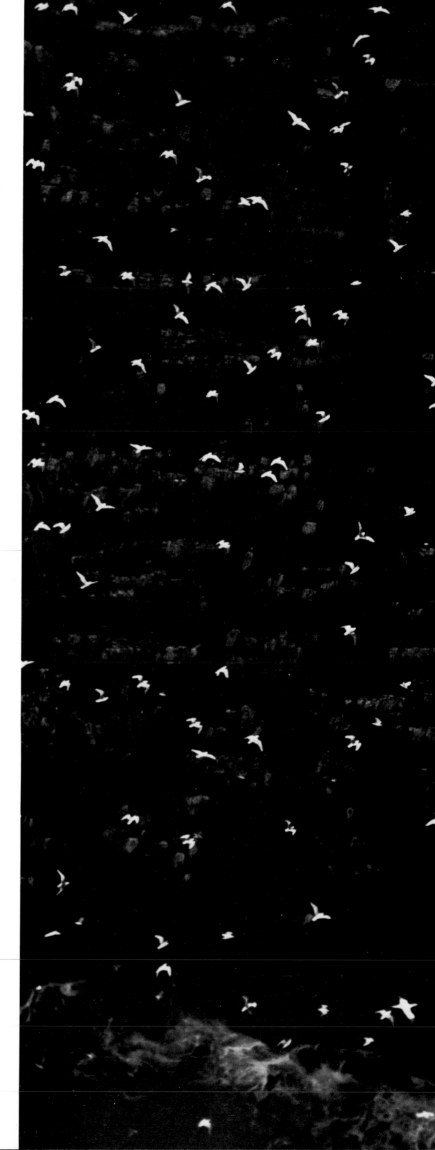

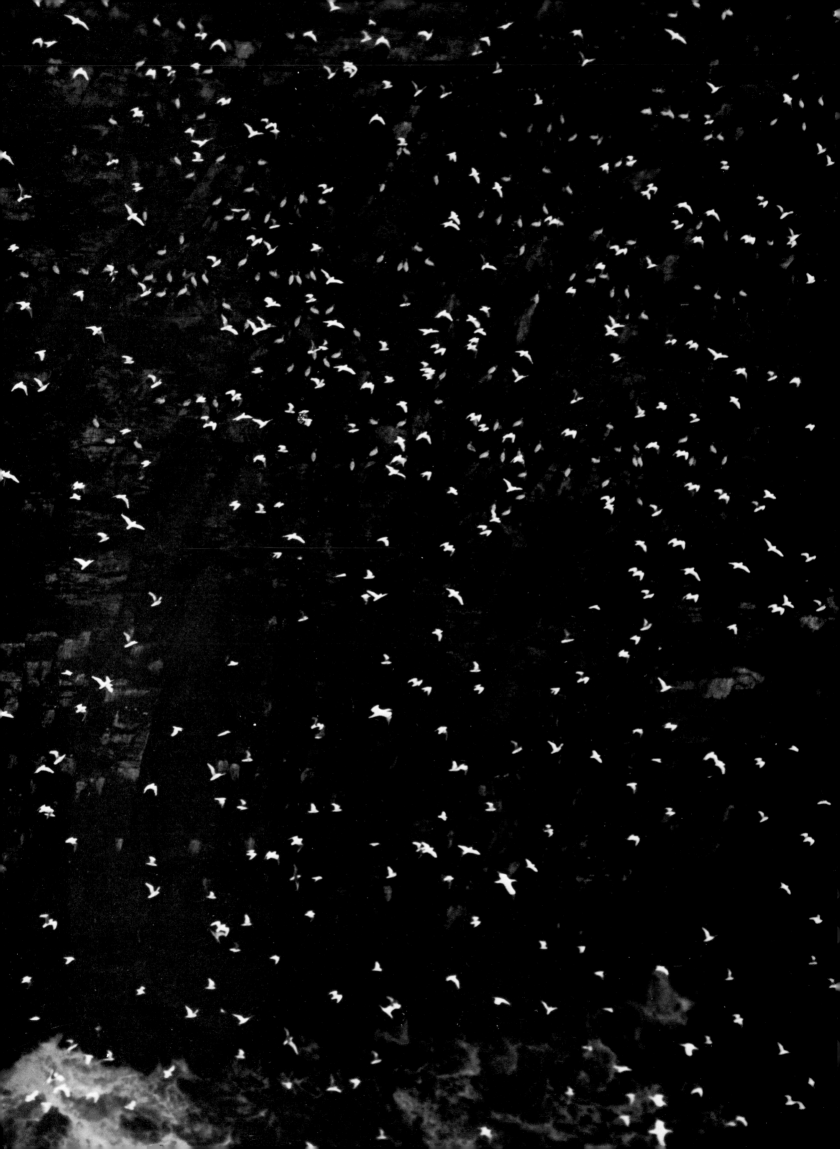

Cabot's news of the discovery of this part of the New World was received with hardly any more importance than his reports about the cod, the lowly fish that soon supplemented European diets as dried or salted cod. The Portuguese earned more from their cod fishing on the Grand Banks (the area where most of the cod fishing takes place, about 300 miles southwest of Cape Race) than the Spanish did from their South American treasure expeditions.

While the cod fisheries were developing into "fleet" operations, Europe came up with another source of revenue for people who fished in Newfoundland waters: sperm oil. It soon took the place of candles and mineral oils to light London ballrooms. And the whale, which had been hunted as food for centuries by the Labrador Eskimos, became important for its blubber and teeth. So large were the whaling ventures of the late nineteenth century that the whales nearly became extinct. Today

whaling is controlled internationally. Seal hunting, another late nineteenth-century industry for Newfoundland, has also had to be controlled.

All these commercial activities brought Newfoundland (and the Grand Banks and the Labrador coast) new prominence, and with it new industries inland. Today the pulp and paper industries, for instance, rank with fishing as Newfoundland's most important activities. But Newfoundlanders still fish on the Grand Banks, and even today the light at Cape Spear is to them "like the rays of heaven suddenly showing through the fog." As one writer puts it, "Man can tame his world of trees and hills, his rivers and his animals, but his ultimate wilderness has never been tamed by man and it never will be. The sea will always remain its own god."

To which a Newfoundlander adds, "Everywhere here I have the feeling that I'm only one step away from the truth . . . the sea."

When the first lighthouses were built on the rocky shores of Newfoundland, the actual construction was difficult because the island lacked the heavy equipment needed to level the sites. In 1897, the Lobster Cove lighthouse (above) had to be built on several levels. But buildings of the North End light on Belle Isle (right) are scattered for another reason: the foghorn building was placed as close to the shore as possible.

Belle Isle

The Strait of Belle Isle is not only an important access route to the Gulf of St. Lawrence, it is also one of the most treacherous passages in world shipping lanes. Belle Isle, which lies at the northern entrance to the Strait, is about ten miles long. The first light, built on the southern side of the island, was lit in 1858. There are now three lights on the island.

The Upper Light, the first built, stands over 450 feet above the sea. It is a barren and foreboding setting. Moss covers the granite and slate ground, although in sheltered places grass grows. Since most of the island shore is a cliff, the building of the lighthouse presented the engineers with an almost insurmountable task. A road had to be hewn out of rock from the southern tip, where the landing was easiest, up 400 feet, with a gradient in places of one-in-one-and-a-half.

Once the engineers had the materials to the top of the cliff, they built well. The fifty-nine-foot tower has six-foot-thick base walls covered with firebrick. The house snugly attached to the tower was built for two families. Its walls are three feet thick, and the whole structure is covered with painted shingles, which resist the wind-driven moisture and help protect the masonry.

Lastly, the engineers put in one of the most powerful lights of that time. On a clear night it could be seen over seventeen miles away. But since the light was so high above the sea, it was often cloud covered, and the power of the light was cut down to a few hundred yards.

In 1880, after several shipwrecks, the government decided to install an auxiliary light, known as the Lower Light, halfway down the cliff and below the critical fog level. A third light, Belle Isle North End, was opened in 1905. Originally an open steel structure, it was later encased in concrete with flying buttresses.

Actually built atop a high cliff in 1858, the light of the first of the three Belle Isle lighthouses (below) was so hard to see in the fogs that roll across the Strait of Belle Isle in summer that another light was built on the cliff face only 124 feet above sea level (left). In winter, the strait is iced in and the weather so bad that the fortress-like stone walls of the tower have had to withstand recorded winds of over 125 mph.

The Belle Isle lights are among the loneliest in the Newfoundland area. To the keeper and his assistants, now linked with radio, entertained by television, and supplied by ship and helicopter, the bleakness and the howl of the wind at night is eerie enough. But the lighthouse keepers are used to that.

Fog is another thing. Some never get used to it. It comes in so fast that when the wife of the keeper starts to hang out her washing on a clear day, she sometimes can hardly see the house when she is finished.

Lonely, desolate, and inhospitable, Belle Isle is still one of the most important lighthouse islands on the Atlantic coast. It is testimony to the men who have served on this granite wilderness that a large number of lives have been saved since it was first lit.

This wooden cross and crudely piled cairn of rocks (above) are said to mark the shallow grave of a man known as ''Mr. Crow'' who helped build the first Belle Isle lighthouse in the 1850's. Right: The two lights — one atop the cliff, the other below it – with the foghorn station between them. Known as the South End Light, the lantern chamber of the upper building is 470 feet above sea level.

On the other shore of the fifteen-mile wide Strait of Belle Isle stands the Pointe Amour lighthouse. From the light chamber, the rocky shore looks as though it is paved with gigantic cobblestones (top). The winter weather in the straits is so fierce the door between the light chamber and the catwalk must be secured by both bar and bolt (centre) to withstand gale force winds. Bottom: When building Pointe Amour lighthouse, all equipment and materials had to be brought through the offshore shallows by rowboat. The steam boiler for the foghorn was taken ashore aboard a makeshift catamaran, created by laying planks athwart two rowboats.

Pointe Amour light (left) is on the migration path of the eider ducks, which helps make the area a naturalist's delight and a lighthouse keeper's despair. Drawn to the light, ducks have dived in to the tower making four-inch dents in the copper lantern dome, and occasionally even crashing through the lantern room storm windows. Below: The heart of the clock-work mechanism, installed in 1855, that once rotated the lens to provide ''flashes'' of sixteen seconds' duration.

Pointe Amour

The Pointe Amour light sits on the mainland of Labrador, opposite the Belle Isle light, helping to protect the same passage. At a height of 109 feet, it is the tallest light tower in Newfoundland.

The keeper today follows very much the same path as his predecessors have since the light was turned on in 1857. His house is near the light and was originally attached to it by a covered walkway. Inside the base of the huge tower, the walls, six and a half feet thick, taper over his head, and eight landings break his climb as he makes his way to the light room. Each landing, like a castle keep, has a window in the thick wall.

The lighthouse area has one of the highest records of shipwrecks in the foggy Newfoundland waters. Since the lighthouse was built in 1855, two British warships have broken up on the rocks nearby. When H.M.S. *Lily* sank in 1889, Thomas Wyatt, the lighthouse keeper, saved several of the crew. In 1922, a British cruiser, H.M.S. *Raleigh,* the flagship of Admiral Pakenham ran aground in dense fog. The ship was a total wreck, and ten of the crew were drowned below with the sudden flooding of the ripped hull. The fog is still persistent and thick. But radar, the eyes of the modern mariner, lessens the danger.

The coast, although a navigator's nightmare, is a paradise to the naturalist who may find there seals, tuna, whales, and the occasional polar bear.

Gull Island (Cape Saint John)

Out of the sea, just south of Cape Saint John, like one of the world's most formidable fortresses, rises a bitter, wind-swept and battered rock: Gull Island. Only half a mile long and even less wide, it humps up to a height of nearly 500 feet. On the top, dwarfed by the huge chunk of granite on which it sits, is the highest light on the whole Atlantic coast, 525 feet above the surging sea. This iron lighthouse, painted with vertical red and white stripes, has a long covered way to the engine room and two modern and comfortable keepers' bungalows.

In 1867, the brigantine *Queen* smashed into the island in a snowstorm. Luckily, she lodged in a rock cleft and all got ashore. But once there, the survivors faced the bleak, howling cold and lack of shelter. When three of the crew went aboard again to get supplies, the ship was suddenly lifted off the rocks in the gale and they and their ship vanished in the blizzard. Completely stranded, fighting the numbing cold and the fear of almost certain death, the remaining crew lived on without food.

One of the shipwrecked, a doctor, kept a diary. On Christmas Eve 1867, he wrote, "We are still alive. We have not tasted a bite of food since we were stranded here . . . my clothes are completely saturated . . . who would ever imagined this would be my ending." When they were later discovered by fishermen, all had perished. Only the diary told their tale – that and the fact one or two of the bodies had been nibbled by someone driven mad by hunger.

A few years later, Charlie Coombs and Joseph Rex decided to hunt birds on Gull Island. Their boat floated away in a storm, and they also found themselves without food and with only a small hut as shelter. Their memories of the fate of the *Queen* did not alleviate the ghostly atmosphere of the area. But if there is one thing a New-foundlander can do, it's fight the elements. They dismantled the rotting wooden hut, salvaged the nails and made themselves a boat which they caulked with oakum and sealed with freezing water. They launched this leaking keg and eventually got back to their homes where they were welcomed as heroes.

Many Newfoundland lights are mounted on circular steel towers prefabricated elsewhere and hauled to the site. The tower for the Gull Island light at Cape Saint John (left) had to be hauled almost 500 feet up a cliff from the beach below. The island itself (above) is a massive, barren rock that rears with brutal suddenness from the North Atlantic, and the lighthouse keepers are its only inhabitants.

Left: The cliff up which the prefabricated lighthouse tower for Gull Island light station was hauled. Below: The rambling frame keepers' house at Long Point (Twillingate) light on the northeast coast of Newfoundland has accommodation for two families and is maintained by the keepers themselves. It is a never-ending task, since the lighthouse sits on a cliff, exposed to the notorious Newfoundland coastal weather.

Opposite page: The gloom of the familiar curving staircase found in almost all lighthouses gives way to a sudden blaze of sunlight streaming through the lamproom windows of Long Point (Twillingate) light. The light is 331 feet above sea level on top of the cliff called Devil's Cove Head, where winds are so fierce that a 200-foot-long enclosed walkway was built from the keepers' house to the fog-horn building, with an exit part way along its length leading to the light tower. The door (left) to the tower itself is of fireproof cast iron—but was cast with panel mouldings so it would look like wood.

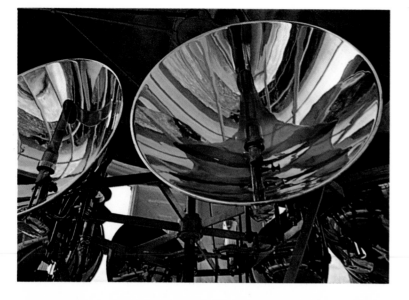

Cape Bonavista

From the rugged headland at Cape Bonavista, where the sea and the birds are rarely still, a light flashes for half a second every nine and a half seconds, warning all ships of the treacherous waters beneath. The light stands on top of a steel tower erected in 1966. Close by, the old lighthouse, boldly painted with red and white vertical bands, has been preserved and turned into a museum.

Designed by Trinity House in England, the old building was framed with strong timbers, 9″ x 9″ sills and 3″ x 9″ joists. Rising through the centre of the 30′ x 30′ two-storey house is the stone tower, some thirteen feet in diameter. Its walls are fitted with fireplaces, flues, and even a bake oven, a homey contrast to the mechanization of the new light.

Inside the tower, wooden steps lead to the lantern on the top. The lantern's rivetted copper roof shelters the prize of this ancient lighthouse: the original reflector lamps and revolving mechanism that once illuminated Robert Stevenson's famed engineering masterpiece, the Bell Rock lighthouse in Scotland. Sixteen burners revolving with silvered copper reflectors once shone a white and red light every ninety seconds. It took the keepers three hours each day to clean and polish the glistening apparatus.

Cape Bonavista has long been believed to be the place where explorer John Cabot landed in the seventeenth century. Top left: The famous lanterns of Cape Bonavista light, which once shone from the great Bell Rock lighthouse in Scotland. Bottom left: Sea air corrodes all metal, and rust seeps through many coats of paint on the latch of the lighthouse door. Right: Cape Bonavista, with old and new lights standing side by side.

Cape Spear

In July of 1835, the frigate *Rhine* was lost in thick fog near St. John's harbour. Several boats were dispatched to search for her. The man who finally guided her to safety through the tricky narrows was James Cantwell. On board the *Rhine* was a royal visitor, Prince Henry of the Netherlands, who later expressed his gratitude by granting Cantwell a favour. Cantwell requested to be the keeper of the Cape Spear lighthouse, then under construction. Witnessed by the governor, the prince signed a parchment document, still in existence, granting Cantwell his request and adding that the post should be passed on to his descendants. Seven generations of Cantwells have tended the lights at Cape Spear.

Cape Spear is the New World's closest point to the Old, and the lighthouse was the first built in Newfoundland. Its seven revolving reflector lights once shone on waters at the Inchkeith light station and were brought out specially from Scotland for the Cape Spear lighthouse. Two hundred and forty-six feet above the sea, the lights could be seen for eighteen miles on clear nights.

The old building with its round stone tower is now deserted. Its duties are carried on by a new concrete lighthouse nearby.

Left: Baccalieu Island light is so inaccessible that all supplies, including heavy drums of oil for the diesel generator, must be hauled up the cliff face by derrick.
Right: Cape Spear light, perched on the most easterly part of Canada.

The circular tower of the Ferryland light (below) on the Avalon Peninsula looks like Newfoundland's other familiar prefabricated steel towers. But in this case, the main tower is of brick, coated with steel on the outside as fire and weather protection. The matter of insulating such exposed structures is always a problem. The house was built in 1871 at the same time as the tower. Until the light was automated a few years ago, its keeper endured the hazards of the ice storms whose coating sealed the house from the chilling wind.

Cape Race

Cape Race is the first land sighted by most North Atlantic shipping to Canada. The lighthouse stands atop jagged cliffs formed of slate in almost vertical strata, a hundred feet high. Its beacon is a warning for one of the most frightening coasts in the world. Fog, icebergs, or storms – sometimes all three at once – plague shipping. Treacherous currents above razor reefs swirl back and forth.

Robert Oke, inspector of Newfoundland lighthouses, said in 1856, "Cape Race Light is a fixed white catoptric light, has thirteen argand lamps and reflectors – burns at an elevation above the level of the sea 180 feet – visible seaward from N.E. by E. seaward round by the S.E. and south to west and in clear weather can be seen seventeen miles from a vessel's deck. The tower is of iron and is surrounded by a stone wall, the space between the tower and the wall, nine feet, which is laid off into six apartments as a residence for the keepers, one partition in each room being a portion of the tower (iron)." Two fireplaces only were provided. And because their flues were so near the tower, the smoke was intolerable. Since the walls and inside of the tower were either streaming with damp or coated with ice according to the weather, a wooden dwelling house and covered way were built for the keeper.

Maintenance costs were covered by a light duty levied by Her Majesty's government on all trans-Atlantic shipping to and from the Gulf of St. Lawrence. The tolls were collected from the ships at port of clearance, the charge being one-sixteenth of a penny per ton. In 1860 the total maintenance costs amounted to £471-10s-6d, of which Canada paid £169-15s-0d.

Even with these lights, shipping was in danger. On Christmas Day 1856, for instance, the keepers at Cape Race were called out into a fog that was so thick it obliterated their light at 400 yards. The *Welsford,* bound for Liverpool, lay on the rocks below. Through the night, the tough, dogged keepers dragged four survivors to safety; the rest of the crew was lost with the ship. In April 1863, the fog was so bad that the Allan Line mail steamer *Anglo-Saxon* went ashore near the cape. While the lighthousemen worked to save as many as they could, the ship broke her back and 238 went down with her.

It was at Cape Race that Newfoundlanders wishing to go to England in a hurry would wait to catch the swift mailboats. Children, women, and even pet animals had to

Cape Race lighthouse (above) is one of the great landfall lights for shipping bound for Canada, but it is also invaluable to the Newfoundland fishing fleets. Even so, in fog, the smaller fishing boats still use their traditional navigational and warning equipment–a mouth horn and gimbal compass (top).

Below, left: The oil storage tanks for the diesel generator are dwarfed by reinforced concrete tower at Cape Race. Below: Inside the lightroom, the influence of the sea is immediately obvious, although the adjustable ventilators were for a different purpose than those found on ships. They were used to control the draught for the long-gone kerosene vapour lights, and needed constant adjustment as the wind shifted.

suffer the tedious and rough journey from St. John's, only to find themselves on top of a cliff, a hundred feet above the uninviting rocks of the shore, facing a single iron ladder down to the pilot ship. Local lore had it that if they survived the trip down the ladder and out to the mail boat, they would enjoy the journey, whatever the weather.

The mail for Newfoundland also came to Cape Race. If the seas were heavy, the mail boat tossed it over in canisters. Any fisherman who presented such a canister to the postmaster was rewarded with five pounds sterling.

In 1866, another improvement was made at Cape Race, to make the lighthouse more readily identifiable. Robert Oke recommended the light be changed from fixed to revolving. The conversion included a new cast iron and gunmetal lantern, lights, and a revolving clockwork enclosed in a mahogany case. A powerful, ten-inch steam whistle was installed at the light station in 1872. In thick foggy weather or snowstorms, it screeched for ten seconds in every minute. An audible range of twenty miles was claimed when the weather was calm; the distance was reduced to seven miles when sounding against the wind or storm.

On July 1, 1886, Cape Race was handed over to the Canadian government, along with $102,895 in accrued funds from previous dues. The transaction was made on the condition that the new owners abolish the levy of this special tax.

The old lighthouse was replaced in 1907 with a lighthouse then ranked among the finest in the world. The tower, built of reinforced concrete, cylindrical in form, eighteen feet in diameter, rises ninety-six feet. The lantern enclosing the lighting apparatus is the same diameter as the tower. It consists of cast iron murette seven feet high, glazing twelve and a half feet high, and copper dome supported on steel framing weighs twenty-four tons. The hyper-radial lens, the largest type ever built, consists of built-up reflecting prisms and projecting lenses, mounted in a gunmetal framing, with four optical faces. The diameter of each is over eight feet. The gunmetal and glass weigh five and a half tons. The lens revolves by clockwork at the rate of one revolution every thirty seconds. In order to get the right speed and steadiness, the lens is mounted on a cast iron table floating in a mercury bath. Seven tons of optical equipment is supported by 950 pounds of mercury. Pedestal and clock weigh eleven tons, making a total of forty-two tons on the tower.

Opposite page: Hundreds of prisms are contained within the twelve-foot-high hyper-radial lens at Cape Race. This is a partial view from within. In 1907, when such lenses were installed, they were the ultimate products of lighthouse technology. A modern light designed to do the same job would be barely three feet high. Above: Cape Race from a nineteenth century chart.

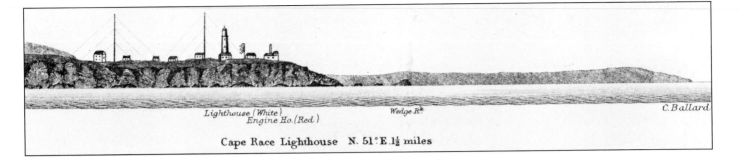

Lighthouse (White)
Engine Ho.(Red)
Wedge R^k
C.Ballard

Cape Race Lighthouse   N. 51° E. 1½ miles

Cape Pine

Five lighthouses had been constructed in Newfoundland by 1851: Fort Amherst, Cape Spear, Harbour Grace Island, Harbour Grace, and Cape Bonavista. They were all on the east coast. The treacherous south coast where traffic passed for the St. Lawrence was without lights. After being petitioned by the colony's legislature as early as 1840, Her Majesty's government finally undertook to erect a lighthouse at Cape Pine, the southernmost tip of Newfoundland, in 1851. Alexander Gordon, consulting engineer in London, designed the building which went into service on January 1, four months before the Crystal Palace opened at the Great Exhibition in Hyde Park. Both buildings were prefabricated and both used the wonder material of the early nineteenth century, cast iron. This material was chosen to meet the demands of cost, quickness of construction, and durability. The contractor's tender read:

For the fifty foot tower with gallery and railing, stairs, ventilators, windows, doors, etc.   £2,192-5s-0d
Lantern and light equipment   £2,330-0s-0d
Freight, shipping, insurance   £400-0s-0d
Landing, hoisting up the cliff, inland transport, foundation and workmen from England   £700-0s-0d

On completion, Her Majesty's government handed over the establishment to the colony for maintenance, intending the tower to be the keeper's abode. If the design lacked costliness it certainly lacked cosiness. In fact, the keepers abandoned it during the first winter, and lived in the shed previously occupied by the workmen. The next summer a separate and substantial wooden dwelling house was built. This, and a thirteen-mile road to the nearest community of Trespassy, cost the colony £788.

Lighthouse painted
Red & White Hor. Stripes

Cape Pine S.81°. E.

Top: Although built in 1851, this cast iron stairway in Cape Pine lighthouse represents the ultimate in durable design; they are still making stairways like it. Above: Detail drawing of Cape Pine light from a late nineteenth century chart. Opposite: The rolling slopes of Cape St. Mary's behind the lighthouse itself are locally called "The Barrens." Near the lighthouse there are fenced-off grazing paddocks for livestock, including sheep and horses, kept by keepers.

Top: An ornithologist has put the gannett population of this rock a few yards offshore at Cape St. Mary's at 72,000. Above: An artist's engraving of Rose Blanche lighthouse on the southwest coast of Newfoundland. Built in 1873, the lighthouse (opposite page) is deserted now, having been replaced by a newer structure built nearby.

St. Pierre et Miquelon

These romantic and wind-swept islands, which have been a French possession since 1763, have a history all their own and a charm that is straight from France. St. Pierre has a superb harbour, large enough to house the French fleet – which it did during the early part of the Second World War.

Proud, traditional, and ruggedly determined to keep their nautical way of life, the St. Pierre and Miquelon folk are descendants of Basque and Breton fishermen who came over early in the big cod fishing expansion when the fishing fleets of the world started to swarm around the Grand Banks. The main occupation on the islands is still cod fishing. Most of the catch goes back to France, although some is sold to the eastern United States.

The nine lighthouses do not come under Canadian jurisdiction, but are listed in the Newfoundland light list. Tête de Galantry, Point Plate, and Cap Blanc are the major lighthouses. Tête de Galantry, the oldest, is now the only one on the islands still manned.

The French even succeed in building lighthouses with that ineffably gallic flavour—and the keeper's beret helps. There are nine lighthouses in the French islands, and only Tête de Galantry light on St. Pierre is still manned. The need for the light itself can be seen from the remnants of wrecks on nearby shores. When the lighthouse was built in 1862, keepers lived inside the tower itself, but later a separate house was built for them (below).

Many Nova Scotia lights are located on islands to warn of rocky inshore shoals. Typically, at White Head Island near the Canso Strait (below), the keepers and their families are the only residents. A light was first located on White Head Island in 1854, but the present tower is relatively modern and is equipped with a light similar to those used in airport control towers.

Previous pages: This view of Louisbourg under siege by the British in 1758 was, the records say, "drawn on the spot by Captain Ince of the 35th Regiment – Engraved by P. Canot." The invading British destroyed the lighthouse (foreground) with cannon fire, and it was not replaced until 1842. Key to the picture: 1–The City; 2–Gabarus Bay; 3–the British camp; 4–The French fleet; 5–Island Battery; 6–Lighthouse.

Lighthouses are so much part of life in the Maritime provinces that they have been enshrined in local folk art. The sign (below), stands in a lane near Cheticamp Island, Cape Breton. The miniature lighthouse (bottom) on a Cape Breton front lawn is similar to many homemade garden decorations commonly seen in east coast communities.

Nova Scotia

The shattered shape of the shoreline of Nova Scotia has been described by ship captains as more dangerous to shipping than Fifth Avenue, New York, to a blind man. "God alone knows how many vessels have thudded into the sandshoals, thrown themselves onto the rocks and broken their backs off the South Shore," wrote Captain Israel Carpenter in 1894, "and only God knows what it feels like to be a skipper at that time when you are helplessly at the mercy of the elements."

On the east side of the province (the South Shore), wild winds sweep bare the jagged promontories and send forty-foot waves dashing against the granite rims of the numerous bays and coves. Up above, on the hills behind the rocks, small fishing villages with bright white houses and gaily painted boats nestle together. Into these villages and the nearby fish factories of the province pours a total of more fish in a year than into any other Canadian region, with the exception of British Columbia.

In the days when they started to build lighthouses in North America, lighthouses were not built only to help the fishermen, the immigrants, the merchantmen, and other sundry traffic entering the province's ports. Canada's first lighthouse, Louisbourg, was also intended as a guide for men-of-war and supply vessels into the docks at the fort.

The English built a similar massive light of "old world designed" on Sambro Island, off Halifax harbour, in that same year. Ostensibly, the light was to guide fishing vessels back to port, but history shows it was also a military light. The light was not, however, always lit; fishermen and merchantmen from the West Indies and other exotic ports of call occasionally had to wait out the night or the fog because of the lack of a light before entering the harbour.

Immigration and commerce soon took their place beside the military machine in Nova Scotia, and by 1790, the province had two new lights. Cape Roseway and Shelburne lights were built in 1788 and 1789. The massive masonry style of the early lights was soon replaced by the cheaper, faster-to-erect, and sometimes more efficient timber-frame type of light, many of which still stand today down the east coast of the Atlantic.

The ghostly sailing ship passing Maugher Beach Light at the mouth of Halifax harbour is the *Bluenose II*, a modern replica of the world-famous Canadian fishing schooner that was undefeated in ocean races during the 1920's and 1930's. The lighthouse, too, is famous as one of the marshalling points for the armada-sized convoys that braved U-boat packs in the North Atlantic during the Second World War.

Basically, three styles began to evolve in Nova Scotia: freestanding lights, lights attached to the keeper's house, and lights mounted in the roof of the keeper's dwelling. Most were made of wood. These three (and almost unlimited variations of them) soon became common. However, although timber was plentiful, it had to be hauled long distances, shipped, and then hauled up cliff faces to the site. As a result, the problem in the Nova Scotia light-building program soon became not so much what type of light to put up, but how to get it up.

Even land lights were tough to build. At Baccaro, for instance, all materials had to be dragged miles down a soft sand beach to the lighthouse location. On Little Hope Island, two miles offshore and fifteen miles from Liverpool, Nova Scotia, $12,000 worth of ballasted crib work was needed before construction could be started. Today such work would run into over $100,000. At Amet Island, seven miles off Nova Scotia's north shore, huge boulders had to be transported and placed all round the island to keep back the corrosive powers of the sea. Piled on one another, they formed a gigantic wall, which today lies crumbled away by the force of the wind and the tides. By 1810 there were at least ten lights in Nova Scotia, and during the next fifteen years this number increased to ten in the Bay of Fundy and eight on the Atlantic coast.

Then, here as elsewhere along the eastern seaboard, light building took a huge step forward. During the big immigration and growth period of the middle and late nineteenth century, the number of Nova Scotia lights trebled. And a far-reaching and significant development came in the fuelling of lights. It was the brain-child of a Nova Scotian, Dr. Abraham Gesner of Cornwallis. In 1846, before the oilfields of Ohio, Pennsylvania, and western Ontario were making kerosene, Gesner produced it from coal, and used it in the new lamp in Maugher Beach lighthouse in Halifax harbour. The light and the new fuel worked so well that the gentle physician made a fortune. He came to own a company with the magnificent name of the North American Kerosene Gas and Light Company, which was later bought out by an even larger company run by a man named Rockefeller. Kerosene was cheaper than other fuels at the time and was later used for many Nova Scotia lights as well as for lighting houses.

By the mid 1940's, Nova Scotia had over 350 lights. Today it has about 1,000 lights, beacons, and buoys, nearly all of which are electric. Indeed, many are now automatic, and their keepers have passed into history.

St. Paul Island, North and South Point

St. Paul Island, a small granite, needle-sharp spread of rocks high from the sea, off the most northern point of Cape Breton, is right in the path of gulf-bound ships. Before a lighthouse was built there, the hundreds who were wrecked near the island used to try to clamber ashore, many bleeding to death on the rocks. If they were lucky enough to find driftwood, they would light a fire to attract the mainland. But each spring, when the fishermen set out from the mainland, they would find at least a dozen frozen bodies waiting for the help that never arrived.

Then one wreck obtained publicity. The *Jessie* was driven onto St. Paul in a snowstorm. A note revealed later that some of the twenty-seven aboard had survived ten weeks without food. But, in spite of protests, nothing was done. At last, in 1835, a giant storm literally threw on the rocks not one ship but four, with passengers and crew. So, two years later, the British government finally built two lights on the island. Both were pre-built and shipped ready for erection.

In 1916, the south light was destroyed by fire, but soon replaced, and in the 1950's was converted to an automatic electric light.

The treacherous Nova Scotia Banks, made more hazardous by fitful fog, irregular currents, and sudden snow and rain squalls, begin at St. Paul Island off the northern tip of Cape Breton. The North Point lighthouse is on a rock separated from St. Paul itself by a narrow channel. It is so inaccessible that lighthouse keepers get mail only once a month – weather permitting.

Cape North

This fine light is set on the base of a mountainside with a gradient of one in one. Nesting on a sea of mountain green, the light is on the Nova Scotia mainland, but almost totally cut off by the mountain behind it.

There is a road, which twists like a goat track up the mountain and around its base to the settlements on the other side. And the keeper occasionally uses it to go to the nearest settlement – Bay of St. Lawrence. Its surface is so rocky that he wears out a set of tires every three months, and in winter has to abandon the vehicle altogether in favour of a snowmobile. Once, when the machine slipped sideways down the hill, off the road, and smashed into a tree, the snowmobile nearly cost him his life.

The original wooden lighthouse at Cape North (seen in a contemporary print – opposite page, top) was replaced with a steel tower (top) in 1908, when a fog alarm was also installed. But the site remained the same — a tiny, relatively flat area (left) near the shore at the foot of a precipitous 1,000-foot-high mountain that effectively cuts the lighthouse off from the nearest settlements, which lie behind the hill.

Country Island

This light station is one of the more polished and painted on the entire coastline of Nova Scotia. A light was first lit on this island in 1873.

The lighthouse is one of the few along the coast that is still a family station. But the present keeper will soon be leaving as automation looms ahead. In the meantime the island is still his domain, and he continues to care for his cows, chickens, and pigs, and to patrol the constantly changing beaches.

Time passes slowly on all island lighthouse stations, and the care of the installation becomes a family hobby as well as the keeper's job. Country Island is, like most such stations, more lovingly and impeccably maintained than almost any building in town or city. Someone – a keeper, or perhaps one of his children – carved this picture of the old lighthouse on a boulder by the seashore (top left). That structure (centre left) was demolished in 1968 and replaced by the present tower (opposite page). The island is flat and there is little to see but the ocean, and few sounds save the companionable cacophony of gulls, terns, and other seabirds. Seals play on the beach that may have once been a great sperm whale's deathbed: a massive whale jawbone, bleached by sun and waves, lies just above high tide (bottom left). Above: The two protusions beneath the fog horns are the ''eyes'' of the electronic sensors that, on ''seeing'' the fog, automatically activate the horns.

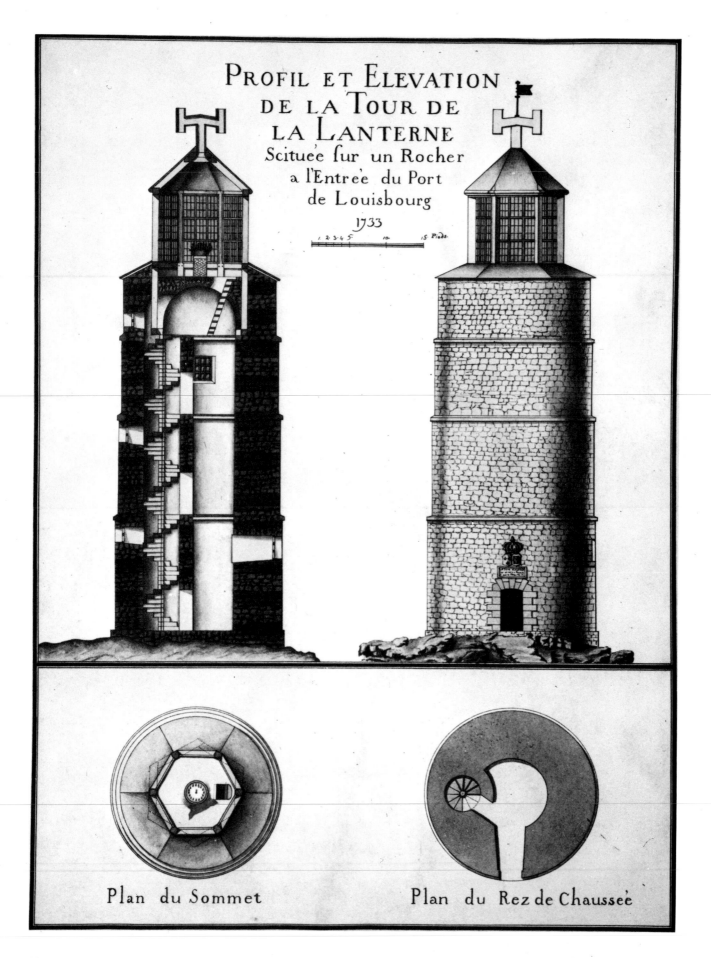

PROFIL ET ELEVATION
DE LA TOUR DE
LA LANTERNE
Scituée fur un Rocher
a l'Entrée du Port
de Louisbourg
1733

Plan du Sommet   Plan du Rez de Chauffée

100

Louisbourg

Louisbourg, the French fortress at the northeast corner of Cape Breton, was the base from which, in first half of the eighteenth century, it was hoped to launch sea-borne attacks that would drive the British from New France. Since the settlements were largely dependent on shipping from Europe, navigation was a major concern and a lighthouse for Louisbourg harbour was built between 1731 and 1734. Wood was used in the first lantern housing (left), which was destroyed by a fire two years after the lamp was lit. By July 1738, the twenty-eight-foot-high lantern room had been rebuilt, this time from stone and bronze, and the oil lamps rearranged so that heat from them would dissipate more readily. In 1751 the light was improved with the addition of reflectors designed to focus the light from thirty-two lamp wicks. It was a profitable enterprise, too. Ships that used Louisbourg were charged a lighthouse toll, and that earned more than the light cost. And then, on June 9, 1758, British siege guns opened fire on the lighthouse and destroyed it. What had been Canada's first and North America's second lighthouse was not replaced by the British until 1842.

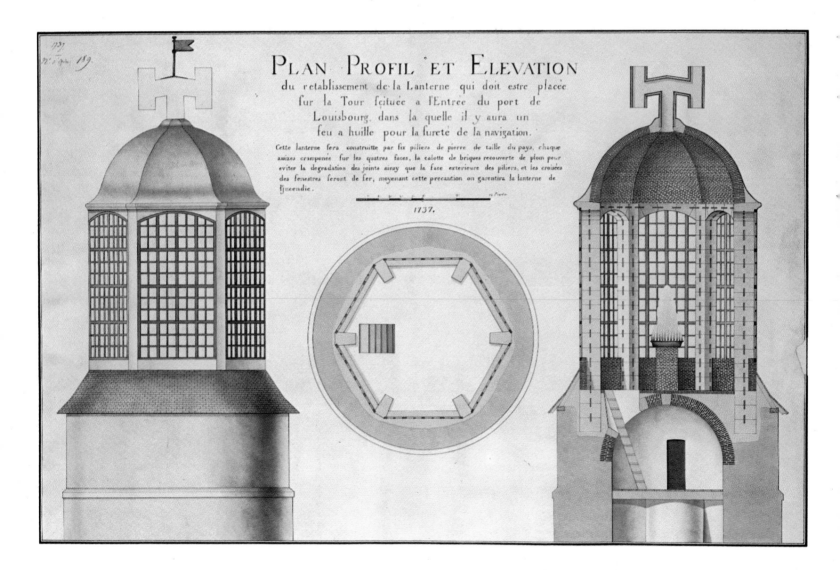

PLAN PROFIL ET ELEVATION
du retablissement de la Lanterne qui doit estre placée
sur la Tour scituée a l'Entrée du port de
Louisbourg, dans la quelle il y aura un
feu a huille pour la sureté de la navigation.

Cette lanterne sera construitte par six piliers de pierre de taille du pays, chaque assices crampenée sur les quatres faces, la calotte de briques recouverte de plom pour eviter la degradation des joints ainsy que la face exterieure des piliers, et les croisées des fenestres seront de fer, moyenant cette precaution on garentira la lanterne de l'jncendie.

1737.

Sambro Light

The Sambro light, which has guarded the entrance to Halifax since 1760, is probably the oldest still in use in North America. The small island of granite on which it stands commands the outer approaches to the harbour and was at one time fortified by the British.

When the legislature of Nova Scotia provided the money for construction of the light, it came up with a novel idea not completely in character with strict maritime traditions. First, a tax was levied. As the tax was on spirits, the government knew it would not take too long to pay off that part of the costs. But another portion of the costs was paid for in a more novel way – a lottery. One thousand tickets were sold at three pounds sterling a piece and prizes went as high at £500.

By 1769, word reached the floor of the legislature of inefficiency in the operation of the light and misappropriation of funds. The loss of the H.M.S. *Granby* off Halifax in 1771 made the whole mess public. "The

Captains of His Majesty's ships are frequently obliged to fire at the Lighthouse to make them show a light and that the captains of the merchant ships complain heavily at being forced to contribute to the support of a thing from which they receive no benefit," says a report of the day to the Admiralty.

The governor put the light under the direction of the keeper, who was not only to levy the taxes, but to bear all the expenses in future. Engineers were sent out, who confirmed that there were troubles with the burning of the sperm oil lamp. There was insufficient ventilation. Black smoke poured from it as if the light were on fire. In spite of modifications, complaints continued until about 1774, when proper administration was started. Shipwrecks continued, however, the largest being as late as 1920 when the *Bohemian,* outbound from Boston for Liverpool, went aground. This steamer, of nearly 9,000 tons, took the wrong radio bearings and made inaccurate soundings. After she stranded on the rocks, all but six people were saved.

In 1969, the original cast iron lantern was replaced with one of aluminum. The elaborate and the intricate dioptric lens apparatus was also replaced by a typical airport beacon with a 500-watt incandescent light. The shingling on the sides has been renewed and some of the concrete floorings, but the light otherwise stands as it did 225 years ago.

The Sambro light (above) at the entrance to Halifax harbour is believed to be the oldest still in use in North America. Though heightened in 1907 (left), the original structure, built on a hill eighty feet above the sea, remains. Soon after the light was first lit, it became the focal point of a scandal. After a warship was wrecked, naval captains reported they had to fire cannons at the lighthouse to persuade the keeper to show a light.

Sable Island

Sable Island has rightly earned its name, "the graveyard of the Atlantic." This island is an inhospitable wilderness. Crescent shaped, it is made of sand dunes, and lies about 170 miles east of Halifax right in the path of the North Atlantic shipping route. It is now twenty-two miles long and a mere mile wide at its broadest point, but is slowly being swallowed by a restless sea. Since 1763, the year it was taken over by Britain, it has shrunk in length from forty miles to its present length and its width has halved. It has even shrunk in height, from 200 feet down to eighty-five in 200 years. The shoals around the island were once part of it and are so extensive that the seas rolling over them make white foam seventeen miles away. The coast is often fog and stormbound at the same time. Fickle currents of great strength sweep around it. More than 200 wrecks are known to have taken place and been recorded here. Unrecorded wrecks would probably double this figure.

Writing to Governor Sir John Wentworth in 1801, Captain Jones Fawson recommended two lighthouses be placed at each end of the island, positioned as close as possible to the fearsome sandbars. In 1802, the Nova Scotian government voted a sum of £400 a year for the maintenance of a fully equipped life-saving station on Sable Island. Thirty years later, Francis Beaufort, a renowned naval hydrographer, condemned the building of lighthouses on Sable Island. Contained in his "Report on several documents relating to the Lighthouses of the British Colonies in North America" is the following: "Nothing however could be more mischievous than placing there a light, though more than once recommended, it could scarcely be seen further than the shoals extend and could therefore always act as an enticement into danger." The island remained unlit until, in 1873, the Canadian Department of Marine built two wooden lighthouses.

The west end light, placed on top of a knoll a good way back from the sea, was thought to be safe from the encroaching water. However, the winter of 1881 brought terrible storms to the island. During one gale, a solid chunk of land, seventy feet wide by nearly 1,400 feet long, disappeared. After the summer inspection, keepers were on the watch for the deterioration of the lighthouse which had been damaged during the winter. Plans were made to build a new lighthouse in a safer place, farther from the waves which pounded closer to the lighthouse. The winter of 1882 was worse than the preceding one. The keepers thought the tower would not hold out to the spring, and they started to dismantle it. No sooner had the superstructure been removed than the remaining foundation fell, and tons of concrete were washed away into the Atlantic.

A Ferro-concrete tower, octagonal, ninety-seven feet high, with massive wing buttresses for support, was built in 1888. The precaution was taken of building it some 2,100 yards east of the western tip. The eastern light shone from a wooden octagonal lighthouse 123 feet high built in 1873. Its foundations were five miles from the extreme eastern tip of the island. The sand bar ran seawards for fourteen miles, but the light could be seen for seventeen miles.

A new steel skeleton replaced this lighthouse in 1917. It, in turn, had to be replaced by another steel tower due to salt corrosion. Today, the two skeleton towers are kept company by other towers, those of the newly arrived oil rigs.

Above: Sable Island. Overleaf: The heart of Cape Breton is the Bras d'Or Lakes, saltwater seas that almost cut the island in two. Roughly midway along the length of the lake called Great Bras d'Or is a harbour the Micmac Indians used to call Abadak–"the place with an island nearby." The harbour is now called Beddeck, and on the island there is a lighthouse, looming over a clump of pines.

The Gulf of St. Lawrence Quebec

Until the second half of the 1800's, the St. Lawrence River remained one of the perils of the sea, although why it should have done so is something of a puzzle. By then, Britain really did rule the waves and had long recognized that as a trading nation she had to make her own shores the safest in the world. And yet the St. Lawrence, water highway to the great riches of the hinterland of the New World, was so ill equipped with navigational aids that in 1828, while the newly independent United States was building lighthouses at the rate of around ten a year, Captain Edward Boxer of H.M.S. *Hussar* reported to the First Lord of the Admiralty in London: "I found the greatest want of them [lighthouses in the St. Lawrence Gulf and River], the navigation being so very dangerous from the currents being so very strong and irregular . . . and there not being even one [lighthouse] in the whole Gulph (*sic*). It was truly lamentable, Sir, the number of wrecks we saw on the different parts of the coast, . . . for the number of lives lost must be very great, and property incalculable."

Until the early years of the nineteenth century, the colonial administration of Lower Canada was hamstrung by lack of funds and an unresponsive administrative structure. In 1805, the Province of Canada did set up the Quebec Trinity House, modelled on the British organization, and made it responsible for navigation down to Montreal. The Quebec, and later Montreal Trinity Houses operated and administered the lighthouses, but their construction was the responsibility of the Public Works of the Province of Canada. In 1809, Public Works built a lighthouse, only the third in the colony, on Green Island at the mouth of the Saguenay River, whose unpredictable effect on the St. Lawrence was a great hazard.

But both the Gulf of the St. Lawrence and the treacherous river, made more hazardous by fog and floating ice, remained largely unlit until 1857 when Hugh Allan, then running his family's influential Montreal Ocean Steamship Company, pressured the colonial administration to launch a wholesale lighthouse building program. By then, there were two lights on St. Paul Island, two on

In winter, the St. Lawrence often freezes into sheets of rippled ice that look like quick-frozen waves. And always, in winter, there is wispy vapour caused by the extreme difference in temperature between salt water and Arctic air. This vapour is as much a hazard to shipping as the ice itself and makes doubly important the presence of Cap des Rosiers (above) on the tip of the Gaspé Peninsula.

Anticosti Island, and one on the north shore at Pointe des Monts where the river begins to narrow.

As shipowner Allan pressed his demands, a pilot's error caused his vessel the *Canadian* to run aground at night on rocks near Stone Pillar Island, forty miles below Quebec. Although there had been a lighthouse on Stone Pillar since 1843, the wreck did draw attention to the need for improved navigational systems in the St. Lawrence, and soon afterwards the government embarked on a three-year lighthouse-building spree.

Even so, to save money the government generally used the British reflector-light system rather than the vastly superior Fresnel lens lights by then acknowledged as being the best in the world. Partly because of this, but mostly because of the St. Lawrence's horrendous history as a mariners' nightmare, shipping insurance rates to Canada remained higher than those for ships bound for Boston and New York until well into this century.

Cap des Rosiers

Four important lighthouses were completed in 1857 for the Commissioners of Public Works of the Province of Canada: Belle Isle, Pointe Amour, the West Point light of Anticosti, and Cap des Rosiers. The latter was designed by John Page, Chief Engineer of Public Works, and built by François Baby, who operated steamers under contract to the government to supply lighthouses. Lighting and optical equipment, made in Paris by Barbier, Benard and Turenne, were installed by French technicians who taught Canadians how to look after it.

The light was lit for the first time on March 15, 1858. Construction had been slow and difficult. Horses and equipment had been brought in by sea, since the roads were dangerous and impassable in winter. When John Page went to see the building in 1856, he praised the contractors highly: "The work has been far more onerous and perplexing than human foresight could possibly have anticipated."

This lighthouse, with its first order cata-dioptric fixed white light, was one of the most powerful in Canada at that time. The original source of illumination was an Argand wick burner which burned porpoise oil until 1868, when coal oil was used. A nine-pounder cannon was fired every hour in fog and snow – requiring about 300 shots a year. The light burned 360 gallons of oil every season – a total weight of one and a half tons, all of which had to be carried up the stairs by the lighthouse keeper.

Below: Winter obliterates almost everything but the light itself at Fame Point, Quebec. Right top: The kerosene tank and compression pump of the now disused vapour lamp at Cap des Rosiers are still in place in the lightroom beneath the lantern. Right bottom: The original Fresnel lens at Cap des Rosiers is shaped like a beehive – this is the domed lens seen from inside.

In 1871 Cap des Rosiers became a signal station for reporting the arrival of ships. Ships signalled their arrival to the station by means of flags, and the message was then telegraphed to Quebec. Although this system was replaced by the wireless in the early part of this century, it was revived in the Second World War to allow ships to maintain radio silence.

The Cap des Rosiers light is now electrified but the original optical apparatus is still in use.

Built in 1829-30, Pointe des Monts Light (right) on the North Shore of the St. Lawrence stands at the point where early geographers indicated that the river itself ends and the gulf begins.

Opposite page: Greenly Island Light has a place in history that has nothing to do with the sea. On April 13, 1928, the Morse Code receiver at the Marconi office in St. John's, Newfoundland, stuttered out: "German plane Greenly Island. Wind south-west. Thick snow. W. F. Barrett." It was the Bremen, the German plane that had set out from Ireland forty hours earlier to attempt the first east-west crossing of the Atlantic. The two-man crew, flying through thick snow and in difficulties, first thought the tower of the Greenly Island Light was the funnel of a steamer. When they realized it was, in fact, a lighthouse they decided to land. They could not see the island itself, but decided that a lighthouse probably stood on land and proceeded to plunge down through the thick of the storm and crash land near the light. They survived, and keeper Barrett's terse message told the world that aviation history had been made.

Pointe des Monts

According to early geographers, Pointe des Monts, on the north shore of the St. Lawrence, was the demarkation point between the river and the gulf. In 1826, Quebec Trinity House chose the site for a lighthouse, since it is favourable for both in and out bound shipping on the St. Lawrence. Using local stone, construction was started in July 1829. When this material was found to be too difficult to cut, stone had to be transported from Pointe aux Trembles, near Montreal. When completed in 1830, the tower had walls tapering from six feet thick at the base to two feet thick at the lantern deck. The robust building was twenty feet in diameter at the top and surmounted by a light brought from England and eloquently described in the Journals of the House of Assembly, Lower Canada: "Consisting of a large strong Polygon Lantern for a Lighthouse, ten feet six inches diameter, and six foot high, in Glass, with strong Copper Covering, Funnel Hood and Nave with Copper Feather and Dart, double gilt and lined with strong Copper, projecting Eaves with scroll Supporters with strong Copper Ventilating Heads and Weather Guards fitted to roof of the Lantern, Copper Pedestal Air Tubes with brass Ventilators. The lantern entirely faced with strong Copper, fitted and fixed with Copper Screws, including thirty-nine Squares of best polished Plate Glass of Double substance as made for the use of Lighthouses and cut to the frames of Lantern with a strong wrought iron cross Frame and Polygon, double horizontal apparatus mounted upon an upright Standard with triangular foot, turned iron collars etc. prepared and fitted to receive thirteen improved strong Silver plated high polished parabola reflectors on improved principles, with burnished rims and supporters fitted to receive thirteen Patent Lamps with Brass Burners inside Copper Tubes, strong brass curved Conducting Tubes, etc., fitted to the apparatus. The whole manufactured in the best manner, screwed and fitted with strong Copper Bolts, Nuts, Screws, etc., etc., painted, marked and numbered, ready to fix on the Tower, will amount to about £960-0-0.

"Extras, Lighting Materials, Stoves etc. will amount to about £250 sterling, not including Oil, Packing Cases, Tools or Shipping."

The preliminary estimate of annual maintenance was:

Keeper	£100	
Assistant	60	
Boy	40	£200
400 gal. sperm oil at 10s the gal.	200	
2 chaldrons coals	4	
cotton, wick, glass cylinders, polishing powder, chamois skin, rubbers, cloths, soap	20	
freight of articles	25	£249
Grand Total		£449

Although later replaced by a steel lighthouse, this original tower still stands and is preserved as a historic site.

Below: Since fog is a major menace along the St. Lawrence, the fog signals along the river are as important as the light itself. These 1905 photographs (below) of Cap de la Madeleine light on the south shore show the fog alarm station surrounded by stacked firewood to fuel the steam boiler, which had to be manhandled up from the beach before it could be installed. The present fog horn at Cap de la Madeleine (bottom) is powered by electricity, as is the light itself. Mariners are able to tell one lighthouse fog horn from another by the frequency and duration of the blasts of sound. The horn at Cap Chat (right) on the Gaspé is also different in that its sound comes from high above any ship in the river. The tower itself is only thirty feet high, but since it is on a cliff the lens is 120 feet above water level and the light can be seen from fifteen miles away.

In some areas the detonation of small charges of gun-cotton was used for a fog signal. At Cap Chat this dangerous material was stored a distance away from the lighthouse in the small stone hut below the ''cat-like'' rock.

The third order coastal light lens installed at Cap Chat in the 1800's still bears the plaque (left centre) of its makers, "Barbier, Benard and Turenne," the lettering etched by the residue of metal polish trapped between the letters. The weather vane (below) atop the squat light tower swings in the wind, and indicates the wind's direction on a dial (bottom) in the roof of the lantern chamber.

The shingles that line the outside walls of the lighthouse at Rivière à la Martre are painted red so that the building stands out clearly against the bleak landscape of winter, when the ice on the river and the snow on land look like a continuous blanket of white. The white stripe on the seaward wall (right) makes the lighthouse just as easily distinguishable from the sea during summer and fall.

The old and ''new'' towers at Rivière à la Martre, as can be seen from this 1906 photograph (below), somehow symbolize Quebec's change from agrarian colony to emerging technological society at that time. Even so, designers relieved the severely functional lines of the new light with narrow dormered windows surrounded with decorative moulding. In 1906 the replacement building had not been painted the dark red that now identifies it as a daymark.

Yet another contrast: By 1909 lighthouse technology had progressed even farther, and the Father Point light tower built in 1867 (below) was replaced by a ninety-seven-foot-high concrete tower (bottom) that could, from its appearance, be the product of the construction techniques of the 1970's.

Father Point

For many years, Father Point, near Rimouski, was the rendezvous point for pilots and vessels travelling the hazardous St. Lawrence River. On the outbound voyage, the pilot was dropped at this point. An obscure 1800 account refers to a lighthouse at Father Point which consisted of a lantern set on the roof of a house. However, the first lighthouse referred to in the Canadian Light List was one built in 1859 at a cost of $1,365. It lasted only eight years before being destroyed by fire. A replacement, built in 1867, became redundant in 1909 when a reinforced concrete tower was built to contain a more powerful light. This cast iron lantern, with its third order lens, is held aloft by eight flying buttresses.

Not all lighthouses are lonely. The present Father Point
lighthouse sits so near to what seems to be a seaside resort
that at first glance visitors may wonder whether it is part of a
seaside midway ride. Even the entrance to the geometric
concrete tower (right) has about it an air of holiday gaiety.

Prince Edward Island and the Magdalens

Although it is surrounded by water, Prince Edward Island is not prey to the same hazards as the other eastern regions. It is sheltered from the Atlantic by Nova Scotia and Newfoundland and is therefore relatively free of fog.

With some of the most fertile soil in Canada and an affable climate, Prince Edward Island became known early as one of the four most fertile areas of the east coast. Since the earliest settlement, fishing has been an important industry. Abundance of cod, smelt, herring, mackerel, and lobsters has brought fishing fleets out of the bays around the two main towns of Charlottetown and Summerside, into offshore waters of the Gulf of St. Lawrence. These fleets have come and gone over a period of 300 years, and the toll taken by the storms and rocks has been severe.

Jacques Cartier, who wrote enthusiastically about the island after first seeing it in 1534, found to his dismay that navigation up its rivers to the natural harbours was treacherous. Samuel de Champlain called it "Ile de St. Jean," a name that it held until it was renamed by the British in 1798, after Queen Victoria's father. The Acadians settled there, and despite the cruel British deportations which took place after the British occupation, some descendants remain to this day. As early as 1803, Lord Selkirk, the inveterate colonizer, settled Scottish folk on the island. Today, they comprise 40 per cent of the island's 100,000 people. In spite of the small population, Prince Edward Island is still the most densely populated province in Canada. Small farms sometimes stretch right across the island which in places is only three miles wide (it reaches a width of thirty-five miles in other places). But in spite of the quiet farming life of the province, the sea is never far away.

Prince Edward Island has always been noted for the wooden sailing vessels and its wooden buildings of unusual architecture. During the great Canadian ship-building era of the late nineteenth century, Charlottetown built more fishing and lumber-carrying vessels than any other port in the area. And because of the amount of shipping through the last century, it has become a sanctuary for old and new lighthouses. Over a hundred light-houses and light buoys came under the Charlottetown jurisdiction, many of them built on lonely islands away from the coast and in the main shipping lanes. The light-houses are in the same architectural tradition as other buildings on the island, which feature wooden frames and wooden shingles – a natural material of the island and well suited to the moist windy climate.

Small range and navigation lights have always been vital to Prince Edward Island and its links with the mainland harbours and other smaller islands nearby. In 1914, when this picture (top right) was taken, the range light on Bay du Vin Island was serviced from Charlottetown, while the outer range light at Wood Islands mainland (bottom right) – also pictured in 1914 – guided boats through the narrow channel there. Left: The rear range light at New London harbour, P.E.I., was built in 1876.

Bird Rocks

The building of a lighthouse at the remote mid-gulf Bird
Rocks, in the main fairway of shipping inbound from the
Cabot Strait, was one of the toughest lighthouse construction jobs in Canada. Chief engineer, John Page,
said in a report in 1860, "I beg to remark that so far as
my knowledge of the place and locality goes it appears
to me that the construction of a lighthouse on this islet
will be one of the most difficult pieces of work that has
ever been undertaken by this Department." The Admiralty
hydrographer, Captain Bayfield, who delayed the building of a few Canadian lights because of his fear that men
would be lost in the construction, described the islet as
consisting of soft red sandstone with near perpendicular
cliffs, well over a hundred feet high. The top could be
gained only in a few places.

The handmade bird house (top right) alongside Bird Rocks
light is not so much a magnificent absurdity as a mute testimony to the lonely life of the lighthouse keeper. Bird Rocks
(left and above) is in itself a sanctuary – but for seabirds only.
Years ago one keeper built the birdhouse in the hope that a
more friendly garden bird – a wren, a marten or even a spar-
row – would nest there. No one now remembers whether one
ever did.

Time has obliterated most of the evidence of more than 200 wrecks recorded on the Magdalen Islands sandbars that sit athwart the mouth of the St. Lawrence. But the fractured hull of this ship remains, a frightening reminder of the importance of the lighthouses on the islands themselves.

The point that the captain seemed to miss was that each year as the immigrant ships, merchantmen, and men-of-war ploughed up the St. Lawrence to their destinations, many many more lives were lost. But Bayfield was right about its being a tough place to build a light. When the lighthouse was finally built in 1870, the site chosen was 140 feet up sheer rock, and could be approached by ships loaded with building materials only in summer.

Even after the lamp was lit, wrecks continued, but at a much slower rate. The fifty-one-foot timber frame building was bolted and fastened to the stone base. In addition, because of the high winds, the tower was securely guy-wired to the rock.

Magdalen Islands

The Magdalen Islands, lying near the centre of the Gulf of St. Lawrence, are joined together by sandbars which in places are only a few feet above the sea. *The Gulf of St. Lawrence Pilot* describes the area thus: "In stormy weather, . . . isolated hills and craggy cliffs are dimly seen through the rain and mist which accompany an easterly gale, and appear joined by long ranges of breakers which almost hide the sandbars."

Wrecks of ships bound up the St. Lawrence from Liverpool became so frequent in the 1860's that over 200 were recorded between 1855 and 1880. Many of them were small boats. Some, as small as Newfoundland dories, broke apart like toy ships on the shoals around the nine islands which comprise the Magdalens.

The islands were first discovered by Jacques Cartier in the famous voyage of 1534. Colonization began with that of New Brunswick. The islands became the private property of Sir Isaac Coffin in 1787, in return for public services to the British Crown. They (and the nearly 9,000 inhabitants) remained in his descendants' charge until 1903, when a private company was formed to buy them. Most of the inhabitants are French-speaking to this day, and fishing is the main industry – the catch including lobsters, herring, cod and mackerel.

Left: Although fairly recent, the lighthouse on Entry Island in the Magdalens is of traditional design. The newer tower at Pointe Herissee (below) on the western side of Grindstone Island is a fine example of the lighthouse technology of the 1970's. Made of fibreglass and equipped with an electronic flashing beacon operated by a mini-computer, it sits in a landscape as old as time itself.

East Point

The lighthouse at the most easterly point of Prince Edward Island – East Point – has a unique place in Canadian history: it is the most peripatetic building of its kind in the country. The sixty-four-foot-high tower was first built a half-mile inland in 1867 and tended by a local farmer. In 1882 the British warship *Phoenix* was wrecked offshore, and the disaster was at least partly blamed on the fact that the lighthouse was too far from the dangerous coast to be of real value in bad weather. As a result, the entire structure was jacked up and moved to the shore, at which time a fog horn installation was also built.

And then in 1908 the sea began to erode the foundations, and the lighthouse was once more raised off its foundations and moved–this time 200 feet inland to its present location. The land around it is a demonstration of the durability of legends about buried treasure. It is said the ubiquitous Captain Kidd buried some treasure near the lighthouse site, and today it is still possible to detect mounds of earth and shallow depressions which mark the places where treasure hunters have vainly sweated digging for pirate gold. If legend is to be believed, Captain Kidd was a singularly careless man since it seems he is supposed to have littered his treasure on every island and headland between Labrador and the Florida Keys.

East Point light is a magnificently preserved example of the wooden lighthouses commonly built in the Maritimes in the late nineteenth century. The functional simplicity of colonial building is evident in the door (left) leading to the ground floor of the tower, and in the massive beams of the tapering walls. Yet in sculpted balustrades and elegant beading (right), there are reminders of the sophistication pioneers had left behind.

East Point lighthouse in Prince Edward Island stands on the third site it has occupied since it was built in 1867. It was first moved after the wreck of a British warship led to claims that it was located too far inland, and was moved for a second time at the turn of the century when the sea began to erode its foundations.

Harbour Lights

The small lights on jetties, piers, and harbour entrances may lack the glamour and excitement that surrounds the great coastal navigation and landfall lighthouses, yet in a sense they are where it all began. The first lighthouses built around the shores of Europe were guiding lights, designed only to lead the successful navigator the last mile or so to port. Small lights, such as the one at Cape Tormentine (below), still do just that. And they have an importance totally disproportionate to their size. It is near land that most wrecks happen, since ships and sailors have always been able to handle the perils of the sea more readily than the hazards of running on to an un-marked reef or rock–or harbour arm or jetty. A sailor poet once wrote: "The ship is your wife, the sea your mistress and the land a treacherous whore."

Small harbour lights are often more familiar to the public than the great navigation lights, which are often inaccessible and are avoided by ships, for obvious reasons. People sailing between Cape Tormentine, New Brunswick, and Prince Edward Island get a close-up view of this navigation light (above) at Cape Tormentine since the ferries pass within a few yards of it.

The unusually shaped Indian Head harbour light at the end
of the breakwater entrance to Summerside Harbour, Prince
Edward Island, was built in 1871. First tended by hand, it is
now automated. Opposite page: The Blockhouse Point light
is a well-preserved monument to its skilled colonial
carpenters.

New Brunswick and the Bay of Fundy

If you stand on one of the Grand Manan islands, a beautiful and rugged place ten miles off the coast of New Brunswick, almost directly opposite the United States border, the horizon seems endless. You can shut your eyes, hearing the surf booming below. You can stand in a fog and listen to the long wail of the foghorn on nearby Gannet as it penetrates the greyness. And sometimes you can stand and listen, as does the Gannet keeper, for the strange, unnerving sound that tells of storms or ships in trouble.

The sea is deceptive. In the Bay of Fundy, a great vein of water between the Canadian provinces of New Brunswick and Nova Scotia, the waters are particularly unreliable. In Fundy they are surrounded mainly by sands. Not one sand, but hundreds of different types of sand, some red, some grey, some donkey brown. Each stretch of beach feels different under your toes, has different smells, different waves beside it and almost every type of countryside behind the dunes and cliffs that surround it.

But it is deceptive. The Bay of Fundy nibbles, sucks, and sweeps at its delicate shores as no other body of water in the world. The phenomenon of Fundy, which has fascinated scientists as notable as Sir Julian Huxley, is its tides which rise and fall as much as fifty-four feet. Huxley wrote, "It is quite incredible to see. The earth might be emptying itself of water. The water draws away as if pulled by some magnetic, electric or unknown force, leaving waste stretches of mud, covered in places with scurrying animal life."

These tides can also be treacherous, sometimes baring acres of the beds of the rivers that empty into Fundy and flooding them on return. Early settlers diked various areas around the Minas Basin, and recent attempts have been made to reclaim some of the flats in other areas. Some rivers are navigable for only an hour a day, and at that with a pilot aboard.

Add to these tides a more than average dose of east coast fog each year and you have trouble. Navigation is, needless to say, tricky. Yet today Fundy is one of the best-lit areas on the east coast. There are over 500 lights, beacons, and buoys at work. One year recently the keeper on Gannet (which is hit just as badly by high seas as fog) went out to haul in his boat just before his lunch

was ready to eat, and when he started back up to the keeper's house a fog had swept in and he had to feel his way by hand along the path. It took him half an hour, and he arrived to a completely cold lunch. At the Machias Seal Island the light keeper once had to wait three weeks on the mainland while his wife took care of the light because of the thickness of the fog. And every spring a priest from the mainland used to go out to the Seal Island light to bury the shipwrecked dead.

But on the beaches, Fundy is a kindly place. Soft breezes, walks along cliff tops among some of the last untouched nature spots of the east coast, give it all an air of peace and gentleness which on the bay itself can change in a matter of minutes into an atmosphere of tempestuous disaster.

Fundy's timbered hills, however, once made the area one of the world's shipbuilding centres. A man could walk the 800-mile length of the horseshoe bay and never be far from the sound of a shipbuilder's mallet. The time was in the 1850's, which was also the first major lighthouse-building period in Canada. The founders of the Cunard Line started building ships in Fundy, and New Brunswick ships from Chatham, Richibucto, Kouchibouguac, and Bathurst sailed with pride in and out of the world's harbours.

The first lighthouse to be put up was on Partridge Island at the entrance to Saint John harbour. It was first lit in 1791, but it went into disuse and may even have been dismantled as there was always (in those days) a running fight between two parties – those who wanted lights built to protect shipping and those who for one reason or another thought the Bay of Fundy shipping would be attracted by lights and drawn onto the sand-shoals and mudbanks. The present lighthouse at Partridge is a 1961 model and the light is the same as those used as airport beacons. Another light soon went in at Campobello Island. Gannet and Point Lepreau were lit in 1831.

On the Nova Scotia shore of the bay (which came under the jurisdiction of the New Brunswick Lighthouse Commissioners), the legislature of the province voted in 1807 the sum of £500 for the erection of a light on Brier Island at the extremity of the narrow peninsula known as Digby Neck, enclosing St. Mary's Bay. The entrance to the harbour here is so narrow that even local fishermen have trouble navigating it. A new light now stands on Brier with a reinforced concrete tower built in 1944.

By 1832, the tone of the battle between those who realized the great need for New Brunswick lights, and

Peter Barnes was a wrecker, one of many along the east coast of North America in the eighteenth century. His greatest crime was committed on Christmas Eve 1793, when he hung deceptive beacons on fir trees on a lonely point in the Bay of Fundy where he lived in an isolated cabin. The lights lured the Saucy Nancy, a schooner laden with provisions, to her end on the rocky coast, and the entire crew drowned. For lack of evidence, Barnes was not convicted – but on Christmas Eve twenty years later, Peter Barnes, returning home from the nearby village of Middleton, became confused by the light of a lantern outside a settler's home, and he fell over the cliff at the very same point where the Saucy Nancy had been wrecked. That cliff has ever since been known as Peter's Point, now part of the village of Margaretsville. The lighthouse built there in 1859 warns of the very perils that Peter Barnes used in wrecking ships.

those who fought them, changed. Even the New Brunswick Lighthouse Commissioners changed sides. They announced in an official report that they were so well content with the Bay of Fundy lights that an increase in lights would "rather tend to perplex and embarrass the mariner on his voyage from seaward."

But when the main body of settlers in New Brunswick, the Loyalists who flocked in by sea after the war of 1776, took ships from New York and other ports, bound for Saint John, they were often landed back in their previous homeland because of lack of navigational aids. Even men like Beamsley Glazier, who sailed down the St. John river wide-eyed in wonder at the 1,500-pound moose and the huge empty manor houses, complained immediately that more shipping protection was needed.

It came after a host of complaints to the British Admiralty and finally to the authorities in Canada (New Brunswick joined Canada at the time of Confederation in 1867). In common with other British possessions, New Brunswick paid for its lights by levying taxes. In 1847, for instance, the Partridge Island lighthouse took £301 a year to run, paid for by the shipping in and out of Saint John harbour.

The growth of shipping, fishing, and, above all, shipbuilding along the Bay of Fundy did much to help make New Brunswick lighthouse protection adequate early on. But build lighthouses as they may, the bay still is as angry under the false front of its calmness and beauty. Its beaches are places of fun and opportunity; of sudden death and of quickening life. Not only for man, but for the countless millions of creatures that live in its sea. It is an exhilarating place, an encounter with the sea at its best and at its worst. So it is with the men who work it. "The sea . . . that's my occupation," one old salt said while hard at work seated on a bench watching the fleet coming into harbour at Bathurst last summer.

Cape Fourchu

Cape Fourchu ("Forked Cape"), named by Champlain in 1604, is an island off the western approach to Yarmouth, Nova Scotia (although the light comes under the New Brunswick jurisdiction). The island is surrounded by three bodies of water – Yarmouth Harbour, the Atlantic Ocean, and the Bay of Fundy. In 1839, when the light was first erected on the island, only a handful of families lived there. All were fishermen. Today, hundreds have houses on the island.

Ships entering the Bay of Fundy from the North Atlantic know they have arrived at the entrance to the perilous bay when they reach Cape Fourchu (Forked Cape) Light on an island at the entrance to Nova Scotia's Yarmouth harbour. The original wooden tower (top) built in 1839 was replaced in 1962 by the present slender concrete tower (above). The island is now linked to the mainland by a causeway.

The fifty-three-foot-high octagonal tower of Swallowtail Light on Grand Manan Island has stood since 1860, but the keeper's house has been replaced. The original smaller buildings can be seen in the early photograph (top). The newer two-storey residence stands on the same site, in a rocky hollow which offers some protection from the winds (above).

Seal Island

Seal Island is the largest of a desolate group of islands at the southern tip of Nova Scotia and is passed by vessels bound up the Bay of Fundy. Before the lighthouse was built, many ships foundered here, the crew members frequently starving or freezing to death on the uninhabited shores. Then two families named Hichens and Crowell settled on the island to provide a life-saving station for mariners. Through their efforts, no shipwrecked sailor died on the island through lack of help. But their tasks were so heavy and the mariners in such distress that they decided to appeal to the government for the erection of a lighthouse. Unusually enough, their wish was soon granted. An octagonal tower of very solid frame construction with a circular cast iron lantern resulted. Built like a ship with heavy reinforcing knees, it is sixty-seven feet in height and has four flights of straight stairs to connect the three landings. The Hichens and the Crowells tended the light in six-month shifts for which the government paid them thirty pounds a year.

A total of 230 wrecks have been recorded around the island, the last being in 1955 when Ronald Symonds drowned in heavy seas under an overturned boat.

Seals bask on these rocks, which is how Seal Island at the southern tip of Nova Scotia got its name. But many men have died here, freezing or starving to death. Most of the 230 wrecks recorded on the island's shores took place before a sixty-seven-foot-high lighthouse was built there in 1830.

When first built, Seal Island lighthouse was maintained by the two families who lived and farmed on the island. Last century the lighthouse was surrounded by livestock paddocks (top). Today the island is deserted save for two keepers and their families — and the widow of a former keeper who chose to stay when her husband died and to spend her remaining years surrounded by the ocean and fishermen's cottages (above).

Opposite page: For many years, Seal Island was home to a small community who fished the nearby lobster grounds. Modern boats allow the fishermen to live on the mainland, using the now deserted village as a depot for fuel, lobster pots, and other equipment. Above top: From the top of the Seal Island lighthouse, the keeper can see his new house and the barn that once housed the livestock that were essential to existence on the island before refrigerators and tractors. Above bottom: The old fog alarm building. The discarded steam boilers now rust on the rocks, but once they were the cause of much labour. When coal ran out, as it often did in summer, keepers and their families had to haul wood from the beaches for fuel. Right: More than 150 years old, Seal Island light remains very much in its original condition. It has been lit by seal oil, kerosene, and oil vapour. Now electricity is provided by diesel generators.

Gannet Rock

Gannet Rock is a mere stone islet, about eight miles south of Grand Manan. It is so small that the ninety-one-foot lighthouse is almost a wave-swept tower, especially when the whole islet is overwhelmed by the sea as happens many times a year.

The activities on Gannet are well documented. The builders, engineers, keepers, and even the shipwrecked kept diaries of the light, its surroundings, and its legends. Even its building was carefully recorded.

One of the people who helped construct the massive stone-based (and wood-carved) structure was also its keeper, W.B. McLaughlin, who kept a running diary of events. In April 1904, he wrote of the construction of the building: "I am now the only living person who assisted in

building the stone wall [or the foundation for the new tower] . . . contracts amounted to six thousand dollars.'' His boss, the contractor, was away during most of the laying of the foundations, occupied instead with the building of a Methodist church in Fredericton. The magnitude of the lighthouse construction, undertaken by relatively inexperienced, though extremely skilled men, was the equivalent of building several miles of super

highway today. The site, chosen carefully by government surveyors in prior inspections, was found to be eight feet lower at one end than the other. The levelling meant blasting into solid rock.

The building stone, brought by schooner to Gannet, was so heavy that derricks and tramways had to be laid before it could be off-loaded. Each of the stones, which were then hauled to the foundation, weighed about four

Since the last world war, helicopters have drastically reduced the time and hazards involved in getting supplies to isolated locations like Gannet Rock. The view from the tower (left) shows how skilful the pilot must be in landing, which is hampered by wind and spray. Gannet rock is often wave-washed in severe storms. That the tower (above) still stands is testament to its solid construction.

tons. Not one stone was dropped, damaged or scraped in its journey to the foundation. "We lived like a band of brothers, there was Protestants, Roman Catholics and Orangemen. All kept the Sabbath on which there was no grog served. I, being a total abstainer," writes McLaughlin, "was chosen as butler and keeper of the keys. . . . I see now the bright faces of those Irish and Scotsmen when they came in and waited their turn [for the grog] . . . on work days the men were served a wine glass of the best Jamaica spirits three times a day."

The work on the lower part of the light was finished by lantern during the night of November 7, 1831. The architect, who happened to be on the island, and his Scottish colleague, the contractor, celebrated the completion by having a boxing match. It is a tribute to their manly skills at construction as well as combat that the wooden structure built on their foundations has withstood the weather and age to this day, although a gale in February 1842 so shook the foundations that a special granite retaining wall had to be built.

There was an unusual fog alarm system at Gannet,

and when the Canadian government, prior to the 1914 war, made a survey of all lights on the coast (there were over 1,400 of them), the Gannet system was given special mention. The early Canadian systems were like giant megaphones which blasted bull-like noises into the ears of the fog. One keeper had a set of old church bells he used to warn potential victims of the fog. Another, a series of drums. Many soon came to use the siren.

At one time the keepers took their families with them to the Gannet light, but the loneliness and the weather put a stop to this practice, and today two keepers rotate in monthly shifts. No such comfort or honourable relief was forthcoming in the earlier days of the light when the keepers were badly paid and often lived in conditions so bad that even the chickens and other animals they tried to raise on Gannet died. W.B. McLaughlin spent over $3,000 of his own salary on the upkeep of the light, selling investments he had on the mainland of Nova Scotia.

Gannet, probably the last tower of its kind to be built, today has a new light which is among the more modern in the world.

The scene above is not the figment of the painter's romantic imagination. Gannet Rock, named after the birds that nest there in their thousands, is one of the most exposed lighthouses in Canada. Even so, the great stone and wooden tower built in 1831 is still in use, and the light itself is one of the most modern of its kind.

Opposite page: The most obvious purpose of lighthouses is to be just that – houses that show a guiding light for mariners. But they are equally vital by day as landmarks, or daymarks, and so one can be readily distinguished from another at a distance, most coastal lights have their own distinctive colour schemes. The markings of Head Harbour, Campobello, resemble the Cross of St. George.

Maine, New Hampshire, Massachusetts and Rhode Island
The First Coast Guard District

We have so long thought of Canada and the United States as separate nations that we are prone to forget that, in the beginning, it was all one – a scattering of communities that represented the tenuous toehold of European civilization on the edges of a vast and largely unknown continent. That some, to the north, were French and others, to the south, were English, and that in time they went to war as did their parent nations in Europe, is a matter of history. What is important here is that those parent nations, Great Britain and France, were the dominant trading nations of the world through the seventeenth, eighteenth, and nineteenth centuries; it was they who sent ships on globe-girdling odysseys, and it was they who pioneered the system of navigational aids of which lighthouses were the first and most tangible evidence. And since, in the end, it was the British who won that particular round of history, it is fitting that the first lighthouse in North America should have been built by the very British burghers of Boston.

Boston in the late 1600's was the major port of what might be called "the new Europe." It was there as early as 1673 – barely fifty years after Myles Standish made his pioneering exploring trip to what we now call Boston harbour – that the first recorded shore light was set up of "fier bales of pitch and ochre," apparently as both an invasion warning and as a navigation aid. The site was at Point Allerton, Hull, an area that today includes Nantasket Beach. At that time the point was, in fact, an island. In 1880, Dutch visitor Jaspar Dankers wrote: "There are many small islands before Boston, well on to fifty I believe, between which you sail on to the town. A high one, or the highest, is the first that you meet. It is twelve miles from the town and has a beacon upon it which you can see from a great distance, for it is in other respects naked and bare."

But it was not until 1713 that the first step to build a permanent lighthouse in the treacherous approaches to the harbour was made. And it seems likely that this step was taken because of the wreck of a sailing ship called *Rose*.

Records show that in January 1713 Boston merchants presented a petition to the local colonial authorities proposing the "Erecting of a Light Hous and Lanthorn on some Head Land at the Entrance of the Harbor of Boston." Edward Rowe Snow, a distinguished historian of the New England states, records that the petition was headed by "John George, Jr., whose father was killed aboard the *Rose*." Whether the first lighthouse in North

America was built because of the energy of a man who had lost his father to the hazards of the harbour may not be clear, but as a result of that petition a lighthouse was built on Beacon Island, or Little Brewster Island, and the light was first lit on September 14, 1716.

The U.S. lighthouse service, now the biggest and perhaps the finest in the world, was born that day. Over fifty years later, by the time of the Boston Tea Party, there were only eleven lighthouses in the thirteen colonies, mostly concentrated in that stretch of towering, craggy coastline south of what was to become the Canadian border where the first Americans settled, traded, grew secure and then rebelled against the indifference and gouging taxes of an absentee ruler. But these eleven lighthouses – some of them not worthy of the name – had so clearly proved the value of navigational aids that when the new Congress took office it promptly made navigational aids a federal responsibility. There followed an orgy of lighthouse building, such that, by 1842, the Treasury Department, then responsible for navigation,

West Quoddy Head is the most easterly point of the U.S. mainland. The present fog alarm bell commemorates the installation at West Quoddy Head of one of the first such bells in North America. In 1827, the lighthouse keeper was paid $60 a year in additional salary for ringing the bell in fog to warn ships away from Sail Rocks. The present red and white banded tower was erected in 1858.

Below: Egg Rock, a small, low island, marks the entrance to Frenchman's Bay. When it was built more than a century ago, the lighthouse was surrounded by an iron lantern, which has since been replaced by an airport-type beacon. Right and opposite page: The first light station at Bear Island was ordered built in 1839 by President Martin Van Buren. The present station is one of the few still tended by a family.

was managing 256 lighthouses, thirty lightships, and countless beacons and buoys.

Among the first of the post-Revolution lighthouses was the one perched atop the lonely spit of land called West Quoddy Head outside the port of Passamaquoddy. As in the case of most early lights, it was built on the petition of local merchants, and politics had a lot to do with whether or not the petition was granted. In the case of West Quoddy, "six leading citizens" of Passamaquoddy chose the site in 1806 and then told Congress: "We . . . take the liberty to suggest that the site on the mainland, the bank being 40 feet above high water, is the most projecting & the nearest to acceptability [and] that we are of opinion that this is the most elligable (sic) and judicious that can be pitched upon for the purpose and that in our judgement the elevation should not be less than 75 feet above the surface of the ground exclusive of the lantern."

Two years later, West Quoddy light showed for the first time and remained the most easterly light in the United States until 1822, when the Libby Islands light took the title. In 1826 a sister light was built on Mistake Island nine miles from the Libby Island light, and although shipping in the area multiplied a hundredfold, the incidence of wrecks diminished the moment the lights were lit. Even so, there were many disasters, perhaps the most memorable of which was the wreck of the schooner *Ella G. Ellis* in 1906. She ran aground on the rocks in the fog, and only the captain, who floated ashore on the roof of the ship's cabin, survived.

Hundreds of lighthouses have been built in the past 250 years, making the coasts of the United States possibly the best lit in the world. But it all started on a two-mile-long teardrop of land jutting out into the Atlantic at the entrance to the harbour at Boston, where America began.

Opposite page: The lighthouse on Great Duck Island was built soon after the American Revolution, and like all offshore stations was a lonely place for the keeper and his family until the last world war when telephone cable was laid from the mainland six miles so the presence of lurking U-boats could be quickly reported. Even today, the Peapod boat, a small dinghy (bottom), is the most common form of transport.

Below: Bass Harbor Head Light, perhaps the most picturesque lighthouse on the Maine coast, attracts thousands of visitors each year. Built in 1858 on Mount Desert Island (today called Acadia National Park), this light, with its attached dwelling, assisted vessels to safe anchorage at Bass Harbor.

Matinicus Rock Light

If not the first, Abbie Burgess was the youngest heroine
of the U.S. lighthouse service. By all accounts she was a
quiet, thoughtful girl of eleven when her father Samuel
was appointed keeper of Matinicus light off northern
Maine in 1853. She, three younger sisters, and their
invalid mother lived with their father on the bleak and
lonely island where a lighthouse had been built in the
1820's. Around Christmas 1857, when Abbie was barely
fourteen, rough weather prevented boats reaching the
island. By January 19, it calmed sufficiently for keeper
Burgess to set sail for Rockland, twenty-five miles away
on the mainland to get supplies. He left Abbie in charge
overnight, since she knew how to light the great oil lanterns and trim the wicks. That night a monstrous storm
blew up. For three weeks it continued, making it impossible for Burgess, mad with worry, to leave the mainland.
Out on the twenty-five-acre island, Abbie moved her sick
mother, her younger sisters, and four of the five scrawny
hens from the keeper's house to the great stone light
tower itself. Within hours, huge seas roared and crashed
across the island, wrecking the house and swirling up
and around the base of the light itself. They were trapped.
At the time Abbie wrote: "The sea is never still, and when
agitated, its roar shuts out every other sound, even our
voices." But not once during that four weeks of isolation
did the Matinicus light fail to show a beacon to mariners;
Abbie and her younger sisters lit and tended it every night.

Matinicus Rock (below) is one of the least hospitable locations ever found for a lighthouse, but the keeper's house,
rebuilt after the great storm of 1857, is comfortable and the
Sikorsky H.H.3F. all-weather, radar-equipped helicopter can
service the station in all but the worst weather. One of the
two towers on Matinicus is no longer in use. Left: Owls
Head Light in West Penobscot Bay, near Rockland, Maine.

Whitehead Light

The infant U.S. lighthouse service was shattered in 1807 by the Scandal of the Whitehead Light, which itself gives rise to doubts about the reliability of the service's records. The official history says the grey granite lighthouse at Whitehead Island that marks the entrance to Muscle Ridge Channel off Rockland, Maine, was not put in service until 1807, but if that were so the Scandal couldn't have happened. The fact is that it was in 1807 that the affair first came to light when a district inspector began to wonder why the lighthouse was using so much oil. He investigated, and discovered keeper Ellis Dolph had since 1805 been selling high-quality sperm oil to the dignitaries of nearby Thomaston, among them a prominent local minister. Dolph told his customers it was surplus lamp oil, but it wasn't; it was stolen. Once discovered, he was "dishonourably dismissed."

This minor aberration of history apart, the Whitehead Light has a special place in the nation's history for it was there that the first successful attempt to harness the power of the oceans was made. In 1837 a unique "perpetual fog bell" was installed. A contemporary writer describes it thus:

> The power of which rings the bell is obtained by the rise and fall of the tide and the swells, which at that place are constant and unceasing. One end of a large stick of timber, near 30 feet long, projects out upon the water, the other end being confined by braces and chains to the middle of another stout timber some 20 feet long. [From] their point of junction a small timber rises vertically to the height of 18 or 20 feet, being well braced to its position. To the upper part of this mast is attached a chain, which, with a continuous rod of iron, extends up to the bellhouse, a distance of about 140 feet. This chain receives from the vibrations of the outer end of the long timber, and a "take-up weight" in the bellhouse, a constant reciprocating motion, which, acting upon the machinery in the bellhouse, winds up the heavy weight of about 2,000 pounds that drives both the regulating and striking part of the apparatus.

The bell was a success. The captain of the steamship *Bangor* which plied between Bangor and Boston said that without it he would have had to heave to in fog. But after a few years it was replaced, and ironically Whitehead later achieved the dubious distinction of being the last-but-one of U.S. lighthouses to be equipped with an old-fashioned steam whistle fog warning; the steam boilers were not replaced until 1933.

In 1837, a unique "perpetual fog bell" was installed at the Whitehead Light station. It was the first successful attempt to harness the power of the ocean for this purpose. The rise and fall of the tide wound a weight-operated spring mechanism that drove the striking mechanism. The bell remained in service for several years.

Right: At the time the first light station was established in 1795, Seguin Island was heavily wooded, which provided ample fuel for the keeper. The present fifty-three-foot cut stone light tower is one of the most elevated on the New England coast, standing 188 feet above sea level. Guarding the entrance to the Kennebec River, the island holds the record as the foggiest location in the United States and its fog signal was in operation for 2,734 hours one year. Above: The prismatic colours refracted through the Fresnel lens light the cast iron stairway.

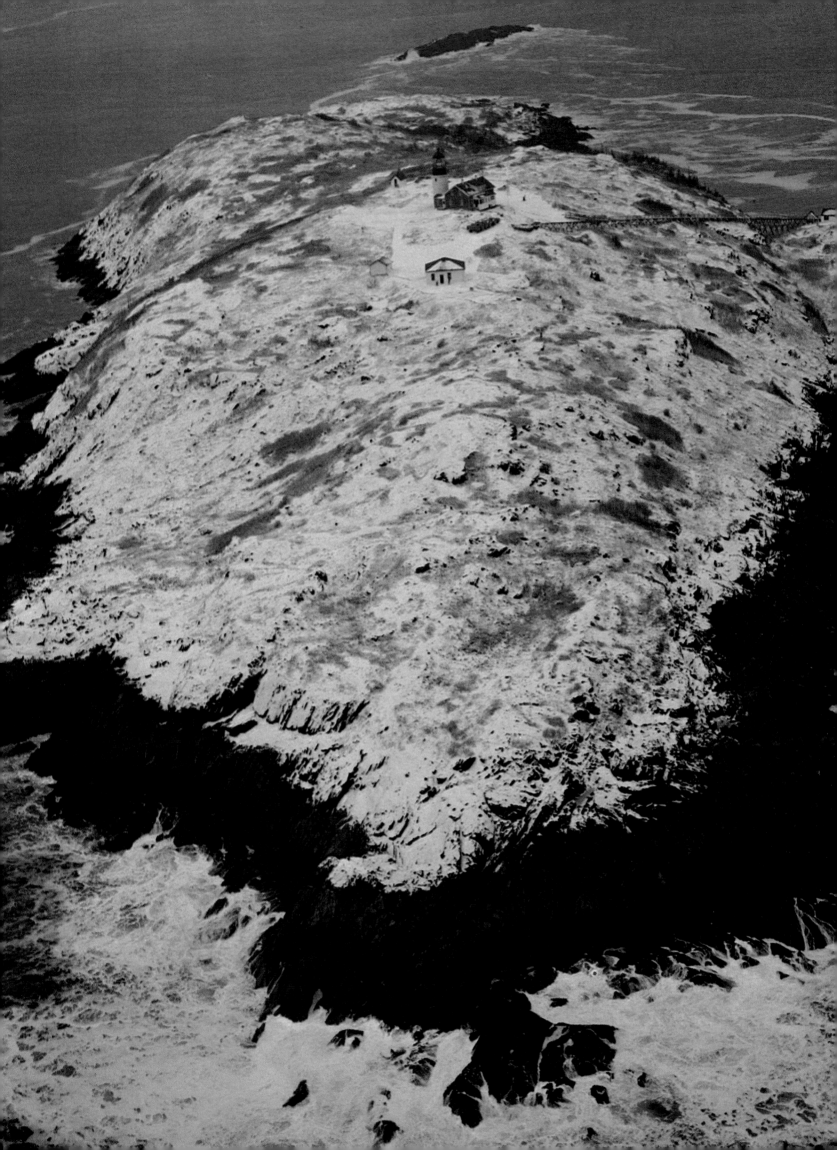

Below: At the end of the breakwater in Rockland harbour stands a building that epitomizes the term "lighthouse." The roomy dwelling with its gambrel roof and dormer windows resembles a New England village home, but the lantern provides the nautical flavour. During the highest tides of spring and fall the building is almost awash.

Opposite page: The importance of the light at Pemaquid Point may be measured by the fact that one of the worst wrecks in Maine history happened there in 1903, when the schooner *George F. Edmunds* was wrecked in a storm because the skipper was only 800 feet off course. The lighthouse, built in 1829, has the reputation of being one of the prettiest along that stretch of the coast, and for years keepers farmed there. It is now automated.

Opposite page: Only one of the two original lighthouses at Cape Elizabeth is still in use. The most recent of many disasters at Cape Elizabeth occurred in 1947 when the collier *Oakey L. Alexander* broke in two off the coast of Maine, and Captain Lewis brought the stern with all the crew aboard in to beach at McKinney's Point near Cape Elizabeth.

Above: The lighthouse at Portland Head was ordered built by George Washington in 1787, while Maine was still part of the colony of Massachusetts. He instructed the masons to use material taken from the fields and shores for the building, as the government had little money. The house with its steeply sloping roof was added later.

Portland Head

Portland Head lighthouse may have been the first to be completed by the new federal government after the American Revolution, for it was in 1787, when Maine was part of the colony of Massachusetts, that work on the structure first began. It was completed to the original designs in 1790, but when federal inspectors found a neighbouring headland shut out the view of the light entirely, the building was heightened and the light not actually lit until 1791. Although the lanterns and foghorn equipment have been changed through the years, the structure there today is essentially that built almost 200 years ago. And since there is a stone on the seashore not far away where Henry Wadsworth Longfellow sat and dreamed and wrote poetry, it was probably the Portland Head light that inspired these lines:

> And as the evening darkens, lo! how bright
> Through the deep purple of the twilight air,
> Beams forth the sudden radiance of its light
> With strange unearthly splendour in its glare!
> And the great ships sail outward and return
> Bending and blowing o'er the billowy swells;
> And ever joyful, as they see it burn,
> They wave their silent welcomes and farewells.

Portland Head light in a storm.

Boon Island

There can be few cases where the need of a lighthouse was so compelling as Boon Island. Nine miles from the mainland at York Beach, Maine, the island is part of a wickedly jagged ledge that juts out of the sea and has sliced the bottom out of many a ship. In 1710, when the *Nottingham Galley* was wrecked there, the crew were reduced to cannibalism in order to survive. Even so, it was not until 1799 that it was decided to put a light there – and the story of the successive lights themselves did more to prove the need. The first was a fifty-foot-high wooden tower, which took three months to build because workmen were repeatedly unable to land there. Five years later it was swept away in a storm. The following year, a stone tower was built, but when Captain John Williams turned up to take the workmen back to the mainland, his boat overturned, and the contractor and two carpenters were drowned. The first manned lighthouse as such was built in 1811, but that, too, was swept away in a storm in 1831. Yet another lighthouse was built, but it wasn't high enough to be of much use and, anyway, it seemed that no keeper was prepared to stay for more than a few months at a time, generally because of loneliness. In 1852, however, a 137-foot-high tower, twenty-five feet in diameter at the base, was built.

Even that massive structure had troubles: in 1887 an entire tier, or layer, of masonry began to loosen and the tower began to sway so badly in the wind that everyone began to fear the light would fall off. It didn't though, and – much repaired – the tower that stands today is essentially the one built in the 1850's.

Boon Island lighthouse (opposite and previous pages) is the tallest in New England, but the view from the 137-foot-high tower is just 360 degrees of bleak rockscape and the menacing sea. However, the keepers are not much interested in the view when perched on the catwalk (top) from where they clean the lantern windows, or storm panes. The massive stones with which the lighthouse was built were hand hewn on the mainland and ferried to the island six-and-a-half miles offshore. There, built into the naked rock, they provide a vivid contrast between the work of men and the hand of nature (above left). A flat rock alongside the lighthouse bears the hand-carved names of lighthouse keepers and sailors who have stopped there (above right). It is a miracle that rock remains in place. Storms there are so fierce that waves toss rocks weighing several tons from one side of the island to the other.

Halfway Rock in the middle of the southern part of Casco Bay is so small and treacherous even a helicopter cannot land there. The seventy-seven-foot-high, white painted granite tower was started in 1869 with an allocation of $50,000 in federal funds. Work stopped when the money ran out in 1870. It was not until 1871 that enough money was available to finish the job.

The lighthouse at Graves Ledge in outer Boston harbour was named after Thomas Graves, vice-admiral of John Winthrop's fleet. The lighthouse is built of granite cut at Rockport, Cape Ann, and took two years to build. It was first lit on September 1, 1905.

The Graves is the last lighthouse on the New England coast where keepers actually live inside the tower itself, and the most dangerous part of the job is starting or ending a tour of duty because the front door is forty feet above the base of the tower (above). One dangerous job common to all lighthouse keeping is cleaning the lantern room windows. At the Graves, as elsewhere, handholds are built into the framework (top).

Boston Light

When it was first lit in 1716, Boston light consisted of candles or an oil lamp. Today, the semi-automatic apparatus consists of two 1,500-watt bulbs, one ready to pop automatically into service if the other burns out. The giant, twelve-sided Fresnel lens produces a beam with the power of two million candles, and by day the lens itself must be covered with a heavy white tarpaulin for fear that it would magnify the sun's rays and start a fire.

Lighthouse keeping is a lonely, almost desolate, occupation. Long ago a historian wrote of the men who do it: "They have neither the fear of the devil nor all his henchmen, but they mark well the waters around them." Between the time it was built and 1939, when the U.S. Coast Guard took over all lighthouses, the Boston light was manned by a succession of twenty-five civilians working for first the colonial government, then directly for the federal government. All spent much of their lives there, and most had their families with them: in fact, one lighthouse keeper's daughter accepted a sailor's proposal in the lightroom itself as she and her swain gazed out across the Atlantic. The first keepers were poorly paid, and generally took the job only because they could supplement their incomes by acting as chief harbour pilot. The first keeper, George Worthylake, established this precedent before he died just two years after lighting the light for the first time. He, his wife, and one daughter were making the fourteen-mile return trip after a visit to collect his pay from what was then the port of Boston when they stopped to visit a sloop. They had what the coroner was told was a convivial hour when "they ate and drank very friendly," before they set sail for the island again. On the way they all drowned. Soon afterwards, former ship's captain Robert Saunders became keeper, but he promptly drowned as well. Surprisingly, no legends suggest the lighthouse is jinxed, though later keepers were reportedly somewhat nervous about the ghost of The Lady in Black. This lady is allegedly the spirit of a beautiful southern belle who, on discovering her Confederate officer husband was a Union captive on George's Island not far from the lighthouse, set out on a rescue mission. She was caught and shot as a spy, her restless spirit frightening (or stimulating) the imaginations of hapless soldiers, mariners, and lighthouse keepers ever since.

Little Brewster Island (below), where it all began. It was here, at the inner entrance to Boston harbour, that the first light-house to be built in North America was lit on September 14, 1716. Later, a lightship (right) was located at the mouth of the outer harbour.

Opposite page: Historians say that at the time Highland, or Cape Cod, Light was built in 1797, three out of five New England sailors died at sea. Lighthouses helped cut the toll, and to avoid confusion the first "flashing" mechanism in North America was installed at the Highland Light in 1800. The present tower (opposite top left) was built in 1857, and is 183 feet above sea level. Race Point Light (top right and below) was built in 1816 to warn of the perilous shoals and sands at the seaward entrance to Cape Cod Bay. Even so, more than 100 vessels have been wrecked there since the light was first lit. The present cast iron tower was built in 1876.

Cape Cod and Nantucket

The parabolic reflectors first successfully used in England at the end of the eighteenth century were slow to spread to North America. Early U.S. lighthouses generally showed the weak light generated by early oil lamps. And then came Winslow Lewis, who adapted the principles of both the Argand lamp, which intensified the light, and the parabolic reflector, which amplified and focused the light into a beam.

Lewis was born at Wellfleet, Massachusetts, in 1770. Both his light system and his expertise dominated U.S. lighthouse technology during the early part of the nineteenth century. The light itself, which he patented in 1810, consisted of a reflecting, magnifying lantern and was shown at a demonstration at the Boston light. There, Lewis convinced federal government representatives to adopt his system for all lighthouses. It was a distinct improvement over older lights and had the added appeal of being cheaper to run. But while Lewis improved the

system of navigation lights, his lamp and his energy and influence were to become an immense drawback. First, his reflector light was a crude affair, not nearly as efficient as those adopted by the British. One expert later said that Lewis's reflectors approached the paraboloid "about as closely as does a barber's basin." Besides which, the reflectors were so insubstantial that they did not stand up to use. They bent out of shape and soon bore even less resemblance to a true parabolic reflector than the barber's basin. Worse, the reflectors were only lightly silvered – yet Lewis ordained that they be cleaned with tripoli powder, a cleaner so abrasive it scraped and scratched the silvering. One British engineer said Lewis's system "made a bad light worse."

Even so, the Lewis system was officially in use until about 1850, even though the far more efficient Fresnel lens lights had by then been available for a quarter of a century. Lewis had been paid $20,000 by the government for his invention, and because his lamp used only half as much oil as the older lamps, he was also paid a proportion of the money saved. He was, perhaps under-

Above: Among the first three lights to be built under the jurisdiction of the new Lighthouse Board was the brick tower at Sankaty Head on the southeast corner of Nantucket Island. Its construction was supervised by Benjamin F. Isherwood, more famous as chief engineer of the Union navy during the Civil War. The light is 150 feet above sea level, and the original tower is still in use, as is the original second order Fresnel lens.

Opposite page: Ironically, when the inefficient light apparatus installed by Winslow Lewis in the Great Point Light, Nantucket Island, was replaced with a Fresnel lens, the lighthouse actually became a shipping hazard. Its light was often mistaken for that of the Cross Rip lightship nearby, and many ships were wrecked as a result. A change in the light signal itself solved the problem.

standably, so committed to his own system that he refused to acknowledge Fresnel's lens lights as being an improvement. At one point he did place a lens in front of each of his lamps, but they were not scientific refraction lenses like Fresnel's, and they reduced rather than amplified the amount of light available.

The record suggests that Lewis's influence over the lighthouse system was due to his friendship with Stephen Pleasonton, the fifth auditor of the U.S. Treasury, and that it was the inadequacies of the lighthouse system under Pleasonton's control that led to the establishment in 1852 of the Lighthouse Board. But while Pleasonton was in control, Lewis was dominant. Pleasonton relied almost totally on Lewis's advice, part of which was that Fresnel lights weren't as good as his own. Strangely, Lewis lost his power largely because of the scathing criticisms of his own nephew, Isiah William Penn Lewis, who became a lighthouse inspector in 1843.

At the time the elder Lewis patented his lighting system and sold it to the federal government, there were seventy-nine lighthouses in the United States, and all were converted to the Lewis system by 1815 – a major achievement even though the system itself was to be discredited in later years. Lewis, it seems, began with the older lights–the Boston light was the first–and proceeded roughly in the order of age. Thus the Nantucket Light built in 1784 on Great Point, Nantucket Island, Massachusetts, was among the first to be converted. The first tower, of wood, burned down in 1816 and was replaced with the present stone structure. After the Lewis light was replaced with a lens apparatus, the lighthouse actually became a shipping hazard: sailors often mistook its light for that of the Cross Rip lightship nearby and many wrecks resulted from the confusion. The problem was corrected with a change in the light signal itself until 1889.

From the moment it was established, the Lighthouse Board adopted Fresnel lens lights, and in 1853 one of the first was installed in the Cape Cod light, located on high land near Truro, Massachusetts. The first lighthouse was built at Cape Cod as early as 1798, but it was rebuilt first in 1833 and again in 1853, when the lens light was installed.

Beavertail Light

Fog signals of one kind or another have progressed from the great cannon that had to be manually loaded and fired at Boston light in 1719, through bells and whistles to modern, complex, automated equipment that produces sound electronically. The sounds emitted by fog signals have produced romance of various sorts. An anonymous poet once rhapsodized about fog horns being "part of the glorious and melancholy cacophony of the sea," and it is said that the ultra- and sub-sonic beeps transmitted from modern navigational aids have often misled whales and dolphins into falling in love with a lighthouse. The full range of responses have probably occurred at

Conanicut Island off Jamestown, Rhode Island, where the third oldest lighthouse in the nation, the Beavertail light built in 1744-45, has been the testing ground for fog signals since the early nineteenth century. It is an appropriate location because the area is plagued with fog, as is all the coast north of there. In fact, the New England coast has most of the foghorns in the United States. Lighthouses farther south rarely have them because fog is not a major problem. The first fog signal at Beavertail was a great bell which was condemned as a failure in the 1830's after the steamer *Providence* ran ashore in dense fog, endangering the lives of the several hundred passengers, A few years later Celadon L. Daboll of New London invented his fog trumpet, and one of the first was

Opposite page: Although a relatively low tower, Gay Head Light, standing on the brilliantly coloured cliffs of the western point of Martha's Vineyard, is actually 170 feet above sea level. The light's life will be determined by the rate at which the Atlantic is eroding those cliffs.

Above: The first fog signal installed at Beavertail Light on Conanicut Island off Jamestown, Rhode Island, was a great bell. It was condemned as a failure in 1830 when the steamer *Providence* ran aground nearby. The spacious Beavertail buildings (above) are now empty, the light having been automated.

installed at Beavertail. It was a monstrous contraption. The largest of Daboll's trumpets was seventeen feet long, with a flared mouth thirty-eight inches in diameter. It was, said sailors, audible at six to eight miles. The Daboll trumpet was worked by a hand pump that provided air pressure. If the hand pump was too much work, Daboll would arrange a treadmill. A greater refinement was introduced at Beavertail in 1852 when a horse-powered pump was used. In 1857, Beavertail got one of the first steam whistles. When that wore out in 1868, a new Daboll invention, a fog signal with a hot air engine, was installed. In 1881, an improved steam engine signal was introduced there, and in 1888 that was supplemented by the new Crosby automatic fog signal controller that ensured the signal was a consistent and readily identifiable series of blasts. Sailors passing Beavertail must by then have been confused by the many different signals that had been used. It grew worse in 1900, when the fog signal was changed again – this time to a new siren operated by compressed air. Lighthouse fog alarms are now equipped with diaphragm horns or the powerful diaphones developed by the Canadian lighthouse service early this century from the original British patent of Robert Hope-Jones in 1894.

Rhode Island's Beavertail Light, built in 1745, is the third oldest light in the United States. Many of the fog signals used by the nation's lighthouses have been tested there. The most spectacular of them was probably Celadon Daboll's fog trumpet, the biggest of which was seventeen feet long with a flared mouth more than three feet in diameter.

The first tower built on Point Judith on the western side of the entrance to Narragansett Bay in 1810 was a major boon to navigation in yet another area that can lay claim to being the "Graveyard of the Atlantic." The present octagonal lighthouse (above) was built in 1857. The care used in its construction can be seen from the window design (top).

Point Judith Light

The first lighthouse at Point Judith, Rhode Island, at the east entrance to Block Island Sound, was built in 1810, and also served as a leading light to the famous Point Judith Harbor of Refuge – a haven for coastal shipping caught in the sudden storms of that part of the coast. It was clearly needed: that first light was itself destroyed in one of those storms only five years after it was built.
A second tower was built in 1816, but it was only thirty-five feet high, and in 1857 it was decided to replace it with the present octagonal white and brown tower. It's a sturdy building and, on that coast, needs to be: in 1938 a hurricane totally destroyed the Whale Rock lighthouse only a few miles north of Point Judith.

Above: Point Judith light is now part of a larger Coast Guard station and the octagonal tower is framed by the towers of a radio beacon. Top: The stubby granite tower of Castle Hill light, built in 1890, overlooks the entrance to Narragansett Bay near Newport, one of the world's great yachting centres. Opposite page: It may look derelict, but Block Island North Light still shines by night. It is automated.

Most of the octagonal stone tower of Montauk Point Light at
the eastern end of Long Island is the original eighty-foot high
structure built in 1797 by John McComb, a pioneer builder
and architect at the time of the Declaration of Independence.
That first tower was heightened to 108 feet in later years, and
since it is atop a cliff, the light itself is 168 feet above sea level.
Today the tower is threatened by erosion.

Connecticut, New York, New Jersey, Pennsylvania and Delaware
The Third Coast Guard District

With Independence the flow of immigrants from Europe to the United States increased, trans-Atlantic trade boomed, and New York became the preferred destination for ships carrying settlers or merchandise. Understandably, therefore, it was in the approaches to New York harbour that the fledgling federal government chose to locate the first lighthouse built under its administration – the Montauk Point light at the easterly, or seaward, end of Long Island. Many others were built around the approaches to New York soon after Independence was won, but the tower at Montauk was the first. It, like the Statue of Liberty, therefore symbolizes America's emergence from a colonial enclave to an independent trading nation which opened its arms to the millions of Europeans who saw it as the Promised Land.

The history of Montauk Point lighthouse demonstrates the enormous importance the government placed on navigation facilities along the northeast coast at the end of the eighteenth century and the start of the nineteenth. President Washington himself took a personal interest in lighthouses, including the one at Montauk Point. And Thomas Jefferson even took a hand in the appointment of the second Montauk lighthouse keeper. Jacob Hand had been appointed first keeper of the light. When it was later recommended that his son Jared be appointed his successor, President Jefferson testily wrote: "I have constantly refused to give in to this method of making offices hereditary. Whenever this one becomes actually vacant, the claims of Jared Hand may be considered with those of other competitors."

Because of its location, Montauk Point lighthouse stood to some extent as a symbol of the New World for almost a century. As Lieutenant George M. Bache U.S.N. recorded in 1838, "[It] is passed by all vessels approaching Long Island Sound from seaward, and is a good point of departure for those leaving the sound." And then, in 1886, it was upstaged by the Statue of Liberty.

The Statue of Liberty was accepted as a gift from France primarily as a beacon, or lighthouse, for New York harbour. In its 1877 authorization permitting President Grover Cleveland to accept the gift, Congress was quite specific in stating that the statue should be maintained as a beacon; and two weeks after the formal dedication on October 28, 1886, it was formally handed over to the Lighthouse Board. By then the flame of the torch that Liberty holds had been cut away at the sides and glass windows had been inserted. Through them beamed a powerful electric light – the power generated by equipment specially built on Bedloe Island (now Liberty Island). The light remained active for more than fifteen years, until on March 1, 1902, the Lighthouse Board decided the statue was no longer needed as a functional lighthouse and turned the monument over to the War Department. Mariners and New Yorkers complained bitterly, however, and the War Department was pressured into re-lighting the statue and maintaining it essentially as a lighthouse for several more years.

When the Montauk Point tower was built in 1797, it was only possible to build lighthouses on land. Later, engineers learned to build up foundations from the seabed itself. Typically, the Miah Maull Shoal caisson light (above) in the middle of Delaware Bay stands on a concrete column, or pier. Engineers first erected caissons to keep the sea at bay while construction proceeded, then capped the pier with a compact self-contained lighthouse.

New London Ledge lighthouse (below) sits on a dangerous ledge in the mouth of the Thames River. Lower right: The Saybrook Breakwater Light (foreground) and Lynde Point light are at the entrance to the Connecticut River.

New London Light

Puritanism and New England have so long been virtually synonymous that it still seems slightly shocking that early colonial churches often used lotteries to raise funds. These lotteries were often used to provide money for civic improvements – the lighthouse at New London, for instance.

At the mouth of the Thames River in Connecticut, the town of New London grew up around a fine natural harbour. However, dangerous ledges and headlands off the river mouth were always a shipping hazard, and a beacon of sorts was set up at the harbour entrance in 1750. By the end of that decade it was decided that a real lighthouse was needed at the harbour's western entrance. The money to build it was raised by selling lottery tickets. History does not record the size of the prize, but it does tell us that the winner would have to pay 12 per cent of it as a tax. The tower itself, finished in 1760, was of stone, twenty-four feet in diameter at the base and sixty-four feet high, and if the lottery was a success the structure wasn't. By 1799 the lighthouse seemed on the verge of falling down. A new tower, eighty-nine feet high, was built in 1801, and that structure still stands. The New London Ledge light was built later, along with the many other lighthouses designed to improve navigation up the Long Island Sound leading to New York.

Stratford Point lighthouse (opposite page) and Race Rock (above) were built within ten years of one another in the 1880's. Today, Race Rock is still a manned light, but Stratford Point appears to be abandoned. In fact, a computer system with light and fog sensors keeps the light showing from just before sunset to just after sunrise. The operation of the installation is monitored electrically at Eatons Neck Coast Guard station, which also operates five other lighthouses in the same manner.

Race Rock Light

Race Rock was a killer until, incredibly, F. Hopkinson Smith managed to build a lighthouse there in the 1870's. The rock itself sits eight miles off the mouth of the Thames River in Long Island Sound between Fisher's and Gull Islands. It is the highest part of a treacherous ledge of rocks that lies almost directly in the path of vessels sailing down the sound itself. At the same point, the sound shallows and begins to narrow. Tidal waters, entering this bottleneck, race along at five knots, with currents of unpredictable ferocity. In 1829, the local revenue cutter was called out to eight wrecks in the area, and the captain reported there had been several others. In 1846, when the disabled steamer *Atlantic* foundered there, forty-five people were drowned.

Throughout the history of Connecticut, the perils of what was once called the Horse Race were well known. In the first half of the nineteenth century, it was proposed to build a lighthouse on Fisher's Island three-quarters of a mile from Race Rock. A naval lieutenant vetoed that plan, saying that to be of value the light must be built on the rock itself, a seemingly impossible task. In 1886 the federal government hired engineer Smith to attempt the job. As foreman, he hired Captain Thomas Scott ("he's a bifurcated sea dog," wrote Smith), and the two men performed what was then, and would be today, a monumental engineering achievement. They first found that Race Rock was not a gigantic boulder as had been supposed, but a twelve-foot by four-foot rock resting on the ledge beneath. They poured 10,000 tons of stone fill over the rock in an effort to create an artificial island, only to find the fill was swept away. Then Smith devised a system whereby a wall of rock was built up around Race Rock itself. Next he built a circle of wood sixty feet in diameter which he lowered over the rock and inside the wall. Divers were then sent down to lay cement directly on the seabed. In this manner he built an artificial island of cement, on which he built the sixty-seven-foot-high granite lighthouse and keeper's quarters. The job took six years, cost $278,716 instead of the $8,000 originally budgeted, and took the lives of two workmen. But since the light first appeared on February 21, 1879, Race Rock has claimed only one more victim. He was keeper Thomas Carroll, who drowned while trying to row to the lighthouse during a storm in 1885.

Fire Island

Fire Island lighthouse heralds the entrance to New York harbour, and at the same time warns of sand bars dangerously close to the surface. The most tragic of many wrecks on these sandbars was that of the *New Era* in 1884 when more than 300 died. Another tragedy occurred in December of that year when the British ship *Charlie Hickman* ran aground. A line was fired from a life-saving gun to the stranded vessel. Soon afterwards one of two boys being hauled to the lighthouse island panicked and fell into the surf. A human chain was formed in a bid to save him, but when just arm's length from safety the undertow swept him away to his death. The present slender, 167-foot-high brick tower, capped in black and horizontally banded in black and white, first began operating in 1858. Prior to this a seventy-four-foot tower stood a short distance to the southwest.

Eatons Neck Light

The perils of Long Island Sound were recognized long before the most significant lighthouses were built along its length during the latter half of the 1800's. As far back as 1799, a lighthouse was built on Eatons Neck, Nassau Island, at the inner and narrowest end of the sound. Little more was done for fifty years, but during the second half of the nineteenth century several lights were built along the sound. This flurry of activity may have been triggered by the death toll along the New Jersey and Long Island coasts between 1850 and 1870. In that time, a total of 512 people perished at sea in the area.

Despite the new lights, the first tower, at Eatons Neck, remained invaluable. The fifty-foot-high structure also proved to be one of the most durable. Renovated only once, in 1868, it is still essentially the same structure as that erected in 1799. Now an automatic light, it houses the electronic master control equipment that operates several other automatic lighthouses in the area.

Left: The sea was placid when this photograph of Fire Island lighthouse was taken, but dangerously close to the surface lie sandbars that have taken the lives of hundreds. Above: Eatons Neck lighthouse, once isolated, is now surrounded by the blockhouse offices and quarters of the U.S. Coast Guard station.

Where Long Island Sound narrows and becomes New York's East River, there are three major lights. Inbound ships sail to the south of Great Captain Island (opposite page) and Execution Rocks (below) and then keep the green light of Stepping Stones (right) on their port side. Built with nineteenth-century exuberance, Great Captain Island and Stepping Stones were automated in the late 1960's, when the light from the former was moved to a nearby steel tower. Great Captain Island lighthouse is now owned by the City of Greenwich and will, it is hoped, be preserved. Execution Rocks is still manned.

Execution Rocks Light

There are those who say that Execution Rocks lighthouse is built on the bones of the real Fathers of the Revolution – and, in a sense, that's literally true because the name of the light is borrowed from barbarous reality. In the early eighteenth century, the colonial administration was often embarrassed by public executions, because when standing on the gallows or before the firing squad, the condemned would often scream out inflammatory and rebellious defiance of the king. Fearful of the effect on the population, the king's justices around New York decided to kill the colonials in private. Soldiers dug a prison pit deep into the rock reef off New Rochelle, and at low tide on execution day, a prison boat carried the condemned from New Rochelle to the reef. The prisoners were chained to great rings set in the walls of the pit, and drowned as the high tide slowly filled the pit and finally swept over the rocks themselves. The bodies were either left there to become skeletons to drive new batches of the condemned insane before they themselves drowned, or were carted away and buried in unmarked graves when the rings to which they were chained were needed for still more executions.

Even though Execution Pit was out of bounds to the public, its horrors became legend in colonial America. Some historians suggest it was the main inspiration for that line in the Declaration of Independence which talks of "the murders they commit on the inhabitants of these States." There is a legend that the ghosts of those condemned to die in the creeping horrors of a slowly rising tide eventually took their revenge on the king's men. It is said that as George Washington and his ragged army retreated from Manhattan toward nearby White Plains, a shipload full of British soldiers sent in pursuit foundered on Execution Rocks, drowning all aboard.

It may not be true, but the building of the Execution Rocks lighthouse during Lincoln's term of office provided proof of just how much Execution Rocks had burned itself into the young nation's consciousness. When the light first appeared in 1867, the federal government laid down unique regulations for the operation of the lighthouse. Never again, ruled Congress, would any man feel "chained" to Execution Rocks. Instead of agreeing to serve for a specified time, keepers were to serve there only so long as they were willing. Should they want to be moved, they could request and get an instant "honourable" transfer "without prejudice."

Under the concrete cliffs of East Manhattan, Welfare Island light (below) overlooks the confluence of East River's Hell's Gate and the Harlem River. The current can run up to 5.2 knots with vicious cross-currents and rough, choppy water. For sailing ships, navigation was very difficult, especially at night. In 1884, floodlighting was tried, using a powerful electric light on a tall iron tower, but this was abandoned after a year's trial.

Opposite page: Execution Rocks Light was the scene of a grisly part of American history.

Since Independence, ships approaching New York have been greeted by distinctive lighthouses which have entered into the lore of the city. Although it is no longer a lighthouse, the Statue of Liberty (left) was maintained as an aid to navigation from 1886 to 1902 by the Lighthouse Board. Its torch was at that time illuminated by electric arc lamps. The squat Robbins Reef Light (below) was known as Katie's Light after its keeper Mrs. Katie Walker who lived there for thirty-nine years. She first came to the post in 1889 with her husband, at which time she had to row her children to Staten Island to school each day. When her husband died she applied for and received the position of keeper. She is reported to have saved fifty lives during her stay at the lighthouse. The little lighthouse (opposite page) that now sits under the George Washington Bridge was once known as Jeffries Hook Lighthouse. Its beacon warned of the shoals off 178th Street until the bridge was constructed. A children's book about the light, *The Little Red Lighthouse and the Great Gray Bridge,* captured the appeal of the small light, now owned by the Department of Parks.

Sandy Hook Light

Those early lighthouses sometimes lasted where many newer ones have long since fallen down. The sixth light tower built in colonial America was the one erected at Sandy Hook, New Jersey, in 1764. Despite the efforts of both British and Americans to put it out of action during the revolutionary battles that raged around there, the masonry building survives to this day as the oldest tower in the nation. It may, however, have had the top lopped off by either George Washington or some British general. An eighteenth-century newspaper description of "the New York Light" (as it was at first known) says the tower was "of an Octagonal Figure . . . the whole from Bottom to Top 103 feet." Today, however, the structure is officially listed as being eighty-five feet high, which has led historians to presume that, in their efforts to put the light out of action, one side or the other smashed the upper part of it. On the other hand, perhaps the newspaper reporter got his facts wrong.

The first white man to see Sandy Hook at the entrance to what was to become New York harbour is believed to have been the Florentine navigator Giovanni de Verrazano, who explored part of the New World for the French in 1524. The most significant visit, however, was that of Captain Henry Hudson in 1609. The English sailor who later went on to discover Hudson Bay (and to die there when his crew mutinied) was in the service of Holland on that trip. Even though hostile Indians killed one of his men, he returned to Holland with enthusiastic tales of majestic forests, strange wild flowers, and a fertile land suitable for settlement. As a result of these reports, the Dutch founded New Amsterdam.

Opposite page: The Sandy Hook Light, built in 1764, is the oldest standing lighthouse in the United States.

Above: The highlands of Navesink, New Jersey, overlooking Sandy Hook and the western approach to New York harbour, was used as a signalling station long before twin towers were built for the light station in 1828. The south tower housed the first Fresnel lens in the United States. When the lighthouse was rebuilt in 1862, it was equipped with two first order lenses and electric arc lamps of 25,000,000 candle power. It was the most powerful in the country, and the "glooming" of the light — that is, the glow in the night sky — reportedly could be seen seventy miles away. The twin towers connected by a building are almost baronial in appearance and setting (left), even to the decorative stonework on the tower (right). Last lit in 1952, the station is now a museum.

Barnegat Light

The first Barnegat light became a monument to the inadequacies of Winslow Lewis's reflector light system, which was installed in all lighthouses prior to 1850. Located on the south shore of Barnegat Inlet, forty-five miles south of Sandy Hook Light, the first tower, which was built in 1835, stood only forty feet high. It soon earned the reputation of being more of a peril to mariners than an aid. One U.S. naval officer condemned it because "when the weather is at all hazy the light cannot be discerned"; another described Barnegat as "an indifferent light frequently mistaken for a vessel light." In

1855, a Lighthouse Board inspector reported that there had been many wrecks along that coast and said a better light would probably have prevented them. He also found that the tower had been built with inferior materials. It was then only twenty years old, and yet already mortar and bricks were falling out and the walls bulged at the base. Since Barnegat was the first light seen by vessels from Europe and the south, the board replaced Winslow's tower with a first order seacoast lighthouse that was lit on January 1, 1859. The last keeper left Barnegat in 1926 but an automatic light was maintained there until 1944. Then the light went out because it was decided that the Barnegat lightship offshore was more efficient.

Barnegat Light (opposite page) was for many years a warning that there were treacherous shoals off the coast. The brick tower, with its walls ten feet thick at the base, supported a light 175 feet above the sea. Constantly threatened by erosion, this well-known New Jersey landmark was carefully maintained until its function was taken over by an offshore lightship. Today, it is still protected as a tourist attraction.

A famous landmark at the corner of Pacific and Rhode Island Avenues in Atlantic City, the Absecon Light now marks a city park. First lit in 1857, the 150-foot brick tower once stood by a lonely coastal village, guiding ships past the dangers of the Absecon and Brigantine shoals. In 1898 the colours of the lighthouse were changed to orange and black, but has since been repainted in the original white and red.

Cape May Point Light

Cape May, the most southerly point in New Jersey, is named after an early director of Holland's West India Company, Cornelius Jacobus Mey, who sailed up Delaware Bay in 1632. Captain Kidd sailed that way much later and is said to have filled his water casks at Cape May and buried treasure nearby. (If legends are to be believed, the old pirate seems to have littered treasure up and down the entire east coast of the United States.)

The first lighthouse at Cape May was built in 1823. However, the sea soon undermined the structure, and it fell in a pile of rubble. A second tower, built in 1847, proved too short to be effective, so the Lighthouse Board built yet another structure 170 feet high. That massive building, though often threatened, has survived. The constant erosion, however, has continued. In 1938, it uncovered the remains of an ancient vessel near the present lighthouse – relics of a ship built with wooden nails that some believe carried Norsemen to North America around 2,000 years ago.

The rubble and brick remains of the first Cape May lighthouse still defy the sea which caused the structure to topple originally. The present Cape May Light aids shipping into Delaware Bay, its high lantern screened with fine mesh to protect the glass from birds that flock to the area during spring and fall migrations.

Maryland, Virginia and North Carolina The Fifth Coast Guard District

For some unexplained reason, prior to the Revolution and for thirty or more years after it, there were very few lighthouses south of Delaware Bay. History suggests, however, that the solution may be found in the story of Virginia governor Alexander Spotswood's lifelong battle to catch pirates and build a lighthouse at the mouth of Chesapeake Bay.

In part, of course, the explanation lies in the coastline of the area. The coast of New England is craggy and inhospitable and is pounded by the legendary storms of the North Atlantic. By Delaware Bay, however, the ocean has gentled and the shore becomes sandy. Fields often stretch down to the water's edge. The storms there, though violent, are less frequent and more predictable than they are further north. Navigation is easier, and lighthouses harder to build because solid rock foundations are harder to find. Several lighthouses that were eventually built on the coastline have fallen into the sea, victims of erosion.

Lighthouse historian Francis Ross Holland, Jr., offers a different cause for the scarcity of lighthouses. He has speculated that the reason may lie in the power structure of northern and southern colonies. He points out that the North was the centre of the shipping industry, and that ship-owners and their allies, the merchants, constituted one of the most influential groups of colonists. It was they who demanded, and got, permission and funds to build lighthouses up and down the New England coast. In the South, suggests Holland, there were fewer ship-owners, who wielded less power than the great land-owners. Farmers, of course, were less sympathetic to the problems of navigation and therefore less likely to want, or to permit, lighthouses to be built. And that brings us to Governor Alexander Spotswood of Virginia.

At the start of the eighteenth century, Spotswood was burdened with two pressing problems. One was the pirates; the other was the perils of Cape Henry at the mouth of Chesapeake Bay separating the shores of Virginia and Maryland. In 1718 he faced two pressure groups of citizens. The first was a group of planters who told him that the pirate Edward Teach – Blackbeard – terrorized and dominated the coast of North Carolina.

Opposite page: The characteristic southern coastline is seen from the heights of the Assateague (above) and Cape Hatteras (below) lighthouses. The foundation of the original Cape Hatteras light can be seen in the foreground.
Right: The Assateague Light (above) warns of the shoals that extend far off the coast. The Currituck Beach Light (below) still operates, although the keeper's house is now abandoned.

The second group consisted of shipbuilders and seamen who wanted a lighthouse at Cape Henry which, they said, had claimed many ships and uncountable lives.

Spotswood was able to get support for his campaign against the pirates, and could thus offer a reward for the capture of Blackbeard. As a result, the pirate was chased, found, defeated in battle, and his head carried back to Bathtown as a grisly trophy.

The governor had far less success with the lighthouse. He couldn't spark interest in the project locally, and his appeal for aid to the British Board of Trade was turned down. The board found that many influential people in the area frankly opposed the lighthouse proposal. This attitude persisted. A later governor revived Spotswood's plan, but in 1758 the British government again vetoed it on the grounds that the merchants were only prepared to have the lighthouse built if it didn't

cost them anything. Since vessels using any light pay a fee for the privilege, and such dues are added to the cost of the cargo, the merchants' opposition effectively demolished the lighthouse before it was built.

In 1773, more than thirty years after the death of lighthouse advocate Spotswood, a joint party of Virginia and Maryland politicians visited Cape Henry and, say the records, "after consuming an appropriate amount of liquor" actually chose a lighthouse site. They authorized work to start, but the foundation rocks, shipped 135 miles by sea, were swallowed by the sands as soon as they were laid and the project was abandoned. Finally, in 1791, almost eighty years after Spotswood first started campaigning, the U.S. Congress authorized a lighthouse to be built. And, in October 1792, with foundations built twenty feet below water level, the first Cape Henry lighthouse was lit.

These three lights in the Chesapeake Bay area have only their setting in common. The delightful structure (opposite) at Thomas Point Shoal has survived for one hundred years and remains the only manned screwpile lighthouse on the Bay. Its charm contrasts with the contemporary starkness of the Chesapeake Offshore Light (above right), built in 1965, which stands in thirty-eight feet of water east of Cape Henry. Its tubular feet are filled with concrete and embedded 200 feet into the ocean floor. The seventy-foot-square roof serves as a landing pad for Coast Guard helicopters. Of more simple but equally effective design is the channel marker (above left) with its battery-operated light. This light, and hundreds like it, is used on shallow inland waters as a navigation aid to fishermen and pleasure boats.

This watercolour of the Thimble Shoal light (a) in Chesapeake Bay shows the original building which was destroyed by fire in 1880. Its replacement was also burned when it was rammed and set ablaze by a four-masted schooner in 1909. The painter of the Currituck light (b) exercised his artistic license by showing waves at the base of the tower. A 1924 photograph (c) depicts the Old Plantation Flats screwpile lighthouse, demolished in 1962.

a

b

c

The Craighill Channel Range lights were one of three sets of range lights built near Baltimore Harbor. A caisson structure was used at Front Craighill (above) because of the severity of the weather the lighthouse would have to withstand. The tiny structure once housed a keeper, but is now unattended. The rear light (left) was painted before 1930, when the keeper's house at the base was removed. Today it also is unmanned.

Assateague Light

By 1825 there was still a scarcity of lighthouses south of Delaware; only one quarter of the total lights in the United States were located there. Ironically, one major effort to remedy this situation – the building of a light on Assateague Island between Delaware and Chesapeake Bay in 1833 – ended in a fiasco. From the moment it was lit, sailors reported that the tower was too low and the light too dim to effectively warn ships that shoals protrude from that section of the coast. In 1859, the new Lighthouse Board ordered the original tower replaced, but construction was halted by the Civil War. As a result, the new first order light, the first effective warning on this shore, was not lit until October 1867. This time it worked: the light could be seen from nineteen miles offshore. It still can be. Today the lighthouse is surrounded by Chincoteague National Wildlife Refuge.

The fine workmanship of the brickwork of most lighthouses has been hidden by coats of whitewash or paint. At Assateague Light the particularly meticulous construction at the entrance to the stairway (left) has been left unpainted. At the base of the tall lantern windows (above) are drainage troughs.

Cape Henry Light

As has been said, lighthouses mark the track of civilization. They can also, like the Montauk Light, be symbols of the stages of development of that civilization. In this sense, Cape Henry Light at the entrance to Chesapeake Bay is the measure of America's independence, and the value of the federal government system.

The need for a light at Cape Henry was acknowledged as far back as 1718, when mariners convinced the then governor of Virginia that a lighthouse was needed to prevent wrecks. For seventy years, the colonial governments of Virginia and Maryland, the local power structure, and the British government wrangled and bickered over the project, but no lighthouse was built. Ships were wrecked and people died essentially because petty, vested interests were at war with one another. And then America won its independence; a federal government assumed responsibility for matters of national concern, and Cape Henry light was promptly built. Its cost, $24,076.66, was included in the first appropriation made for lighthouses by the new Congress on December 18, 1789.

Builders of the octagonal tower were the first to run into the problem that would beset all engineers who built such structures along that coast in later years – sand. They found they had to dig twenty feet for an adequate foundation. And after the ninety-foot-high sandstone tower was finished in 1792, sand still remained a problem. Six years later an inspection report on the tower said: "The Light House was built upon the highest hill at the Cape. At present a mound of sand surrounds the buildings which overlap the keeper's dwelling and has buried his kitchen to the eaves."

In 1872, it was announced that the lighthouse was collapsing and might blow over in a heavy gale; therefore, in 1875 the federal government spent $125,000 to build a new cast-iron lighthouse 240 feet southwest of the old tower. When, on December 15, 1881, the new Cape Henry light was first lit, everyone half-expected the old tower to promptly fall down. It didn't. In fact, it is still standing – and is a much-visited historical monument.

The first Cape Henry lighthouse (above right) is now a historic landmark. It was replaced in 1881 by the present Cape Henry Light (below right) with its distinctive paintwork.

Cape Henry lighthouse displays a marriage of aesthetics and function rarely seen in utilitarian structures built by economy-conscious governments. The best example of this is undoubtedly the ornately patterned, multi-coloured floor at the entrance to the lighthouse — the sort of thing more to be expected in the hallway of a tycoon's mansion.

The Cape Henry staircase has 180 steps, ascending the six storeys. At the top is a service room, above which is the watch room and then the lantern. The tower was built in sections of two-inch-thick cast iron which were bolted together, then lined first with masonry and then sheet iron. The weight of the ironwork was estimated at 1,700,000 pounds, including 7,000 pounds of bolts.

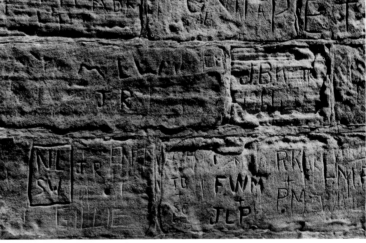

The entrance and base windows (left, above and below) of the Cape Henry lighthouse are surmounted by segmental pediments and elaborate moulding. The date above the door records the year construction was begun. The ground floor columns and interior walls were lined with iron 3/8 of an inch in thickness. The niches in the walls (top) held oil drums. The sandstone blocks (above) of the old Cape Henry tower have been carved by visitors.

Currituck Beach Light

By the 1870's there was, in seaman's terms, only one dark spot remaining along the south Atlantic coast, and that was between Cape Henry in the north and Bodie Island in the south. The two lights are eighty miles apart. But since each light can only be seen at a distance of nineteen miles, an area of forty miles remained in the middle where no light was visible either north or south. What made this bad situation worse was the fact that many southbound ships sailed close inshore to avoid meeting the Gulf Stream, which flows northward. As a result, the Lighthouse Board was told in 1873, many ships and lives had been lost in this forty-mile stretch of darkness.

Whale's Head Hill on Currituck Beach, North Carolina, was chosen as the halfway point between Point Henry and Bodie Island. When the light was put in operation in 1874, the Atlantic coast of North America was lit from north to south. A first-order light was located 158 feet above sea level, and its beams could be seen for nineteen miles in either direction, thus eliminating the forty-mile blind spot.

The massive brick Currituck Beach lighthouse (top) is supported underground on piles with heavy timber cribbing for foundation on the sandy terrain (left), which can be seen from the tower. Within the tower, the steps (above) divide around a cistern built into the base of the lighthouse.

The now abandoned life-saving station on Corolla Beach with Currituck Beach light in the background. At one time such stations were a familiar sight on the Outer Banks. From this building a watch was kept on all shipping in the vicinity. The old Life Saving Service is now a part of the U.S. Coast Guard, and its stations fell into disuse with the advent of fast, sea-going motorboats, amphibious vehicles, and rescue helicopters.

The entrance to the Currituck tower (below) is bigger — and certainly more charming — than those usually built last century. It served as a workshop and housed storage tanks for oil that had to be carried up the 150-foot-high staircase (opposite page). Steel was used in the interior of tower lighthouses not only because it is fireproof, but also because such staircases as this one contributed to the strength and durability of the building.

Cape Hatteras Light

Below the southern lip of the mouth of Chesapeake Bay lies a geological freak. A thin sliver of land reaches out into the Atlantic and encloses a body of water known as Pamlico Sound. Stretching from the mouth of the bay south to Cape Lookout in North Carolina, this sliver of land is, in fact, three eel-shaped islands that form a reef faced by great swathes of golden sands known as the Barrier Beaches. Cape Hatteras Island is the middle of the three. On it sits the great Cape Hatteras lighthouse, a candy-striped obelisk which demonstrates the importance of giving all major lights a distinctive look so they are effective day marks for navigation. The building was constructed at the end of the last century partly because of one of the most harrowing stories of shipwreck and disaster in the annals of the sea.

The first recorded wreck in the area of Cape Hatteras took place in 1526. Since then more than 2,300 wrecks and founderings have been recorded there, and the records themselves are incomplete. The story of what happened to the brig *Tyrrel* and her crew, however, is well recorded. The *Tyrrel* set sail from New York bound for Antigua on June 28, 1759. Three days later, in a series of sudden squalls, the *Tyrrel* capsized, but remained afloat on her beam ends. The one lifeboat floated upside down in the water nearby.

The crew spent hours righting the nineteen-foot lifeboat, only to find it was awash to the gunwale. Only the cabin boy was light enough to risk climbing aboard, and he bailed the lifeboat until it was dry enough for the seventeen grown men of the crew to board her. Then, paddling with their hands and bits of floating timber, they hunted around until they found the rudder, oars, and tiller which had been carried away in the squall. They had one biscuit among them, and no fresh water. The compass was out of order. They had no sail. They were not sure where they were. And soon it was dark.

What is important here is that a subsequent inquiry demonstrated that if there had been a light at Cape Hatteras the men would have seen it that first night and been able to row to shore and safety. Instead, they headed in the wrong direction and later were swept out to sea, where the small boat was captured by the Gulf Stream and swept northward.

Ten days later the first man died. By July 15, there were just three men left alive: the captain, the boatswain, and first mate Thomas Purnell. The cabin boy had been the last to die, and the three men agreed to eat his body. They tried, but found they couldn't swallow. Three days later, only Thomas Purnell was left, except that he was more dead than alive himself. On July 24, having been twenty-three days without food or water, Purnell was found by a passing merchantman. By then the lifeboat had been swept so far north that he was near Marblehead, Massachusetts. Purnell lived, and because he did, the story of the *Tyrrel* and the fate of the sixteen men who died received great publicity. It was then that a

When built in 1871, Cape Hatteras Light, 193 feet high, was the tallest brick lighthouse in the world, and today remains the highest structure of its kind in North America. Its distinctive stripes make it a valuable daymark for sailors. And although lighthouses have traditionally been severely functional buildings, the decorative architecture of the time was reflected in the iron railings of the catwalk around the lantern itself (opposite right).

public campaign began to have a lighthouse built on Cape Hatteras.

That, however, was in the mid 1700's, when America was still ruled by a colonial administration largely indifferent to public pressures. It was not until Independence and the year 1803 that a lighthouse ninety feet high was finally lit on Cape Hatteras. Even it didn't end the toll of the Barrier Beaches and nearby hazards, however. Four years later, a hurricane put the light out. When the storm passed, the cape was littered with wrecks.

By 1816, there were so many shipwrecks that mariners began to voice suspicions about "mooncussers and wreckers" deliberately decoying vessels onto the reefs. They also suggested that this was only possible because the lighthouse keeper of the time was in cahoots with the wreckers and at times would let his light go out so the decoy tricks could work. The keeper was replaced, but it seems the practice of letting the light go out from time to time continued because ships continued to pile up on the reefs to be plundered. In 1851, a naval captain publicly said: "Cape Hatteras Light, the most important on our coast, is without doubt the worst light in the world."

In 1854, the height of the tower was increased from ninety to 150 feet, and a new first order Fresnel lens installed. But that wasn't enough to make Cape Hatteras safe. In 1871 a new tower of granite, bricks, and iron was built 225 feet above the sea. It was, and remains, the highest brick lighthouse ever built in the United States, and is in a sense a monument to the men of the *Tyrrel.*

Cape Hatteras Island is a low-lying sandbar, and by 1898, when the picture below was taken, the original beach was seriously eroded, and by 1935 it had disappeared so that the high tide reached the tower itself. The building was abandoned, a substitute light being erected nearby. Then retaining walls were built to reclaim the eroded beach, and by 1950, when the tower was once more 900 feet inland at low tide, the light was re-lit.

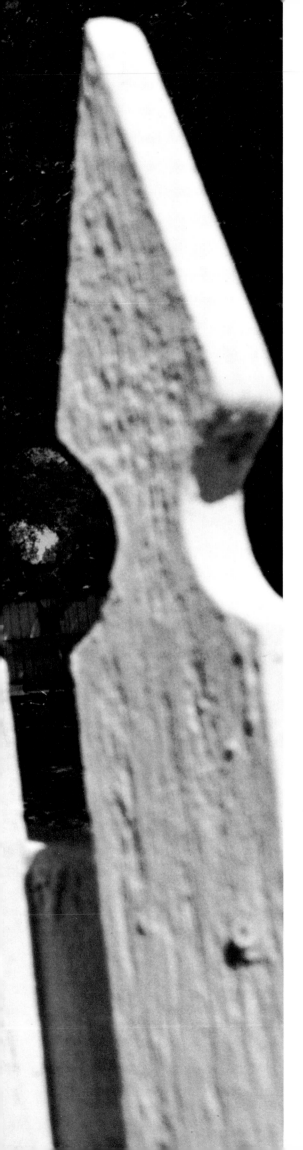

Ocracoke Light

The shifting sands of the North Carolina Coastline left the first of two lighthouses on Shell Castle Island at the entrance to Ocracoke harbour so high and dry that it became valueless as a navigational aid. The first light was built in 1798 near where the pirate Blackbeard, otherwise Edward Teach, once lived, and the man who sold the land to the government did so with the proviso that "no goods should be stored, no tavern kept, no spirits retailed . . . and that no person should reside or make it a stand to pilot or lighter vessels." By 1820, the shifting sands had built up around the lighthouse so that it was now a mile away from the channel it was supposed to mark. In 1822 the old structure was abandoned and the present seventy-six-foot-high lighthouse lit for the first time, and even though the channel has shifted slightly since then, improvements in light technology have meant the lighthouse is still efficient. One of the oldest lights on the Atlantic coast, the tower is recognizable as a daymark by its single shaft of white painted masonry jutting up from the sandbar island. In the early days the lighthouse keepers painted it with a whitewash made to this recipe supplied by the U.S. Lighthouse Board: "Slake half a bushel of unslaked lime with boiling water, keeping it covered during the process. Strain it and add a peck of salt, dissolve in warm water; three pounds of ground rice put in boiling water, and boil to a thin paste; half a pound of powdered Spanish whiting, and a pound of clear glue, dissolved in warm water; mix these well together, and let the mixture stand for several days. Keep the wash thus prepared in a kettle or portable furnace, and when used put it on as hot as possible, with painters or whitewash brushes."

Cape Lookout Light

The failure of colonial administrations to build more lighthouses is the more surprising the longer one studies the hazards along the south Atlantic coast. Cape Lookout, for example, was listed on some early maps as "Promontorium tremendum," which sailors later translated to mean "Horrible Headland." Shoals extend offshore for ten miles or more, and many ships running for the protection of the harbour behind the point foundered there before the first lighthouse was built and lit in 1812. It was reported to consist of two towers, "the inside one of brick; the outside one is a wooden framed building, boarded and shingled, and painted in red and white strips horizontally." Ninety-six feet high, the first tower proved hard to see at dusk and dawn, and between 1856 and 1859 a new 150-foot-high tower was built. In 1873, to improve the value of the Cape Lookout light as a day mark, it was painted in black and white diamond pattern, which prompted a settlement on nearby Shackleford Banks to name itself Diamond City.

Lighthouses have always been expensive to build and maintain. The first lighthouse at Cape Lookout cost $20,678.54 to build in 1812, when the dollar was worth considerably more than it is today. The present taller tower with its giant first order Fresnel lens (opposite) was built in the late 1850's and even then cost $45,000. And the last time the tower had a paint job, in 1968, the bill was $9,444, which included partly redecorating the interior.

South Carolina, Georgia and Florida
The Seventh Coast Guard District

Two great mysteries of nature create unique navigational problems and perils south of the point where Virginia and North Carolina belly out into the Atlantic. The great Gulf Stream is one; the Labrador Current the other. The Gulf Stream, which swirls inexorably up from the Gulf of Mexico and surges north and east to the Arctic and Europe, is actually visible a few miles off the shores of Florida, Georgia, and North and South Carolina until it reaches Cape Hatteras, where it turns away from the coast. It is prevented from washing the coastline by the colder Labrador Current, which heads in the opposite direction toward the Equator, hugging the shoreline of the southern states. Since the days of the Spanish treasure galleons, northbound ships have sought out the Gulf Stream, which moves at about four knots and helps them on their way. Southbound ships, on the other hand, avoid the stream and seek out the inshore Labrador Current that carries them along in the right direction.

Since the coast south of the Carolinas is littered with shoals and reefs and islands of shifting sands, there were countless wrecks in the colonial days and in the early years of the Union. The most southerly part of the area – Florida – was also paradise for pirates who found it a hiding place impenetrable by naval ships whose officers were less familiar with the largely uncharted coast.

The colonial governments built only two lighthouses prior to the Revolution – the one at the entrance to Charleston harbour and one at Tybee Island at the mouth of the Savannah River, Georgia, and that wasn't actually built as a lighthouse. Thus, as civilization spread southward there was an urgent need for more navigational aids. And when, in 1821, the fledgling federal government took control of what is now the state of Florida and coastal trade increased, there was even greater demand for lighthouses. But how and where to build them?

The coast itself was flat and sandy, and the offshore and barrier reefs, which offered the greatest peril to southbound ships using the Labrador Current, were constantly eroded by the sea, often disappearing in the space of one winter. At first, the federal government always elected to build the traditional towers of tapering masonry, and off South Carolina and Georgia it often

worked. When it didn't, the results were disastrous. The second lighthouse at Cape Romain, South Carolina, for instance, was built in 1858, began to crack in 1869, and by 1873 was reported to have settled "twenty-three-and-a-half inches from the vertical." This tilting continued through the years, but the leaning tower of Cape Romain still stands — lightless now.

Farther south, the problems increase. The first lighthouse built at Sand Key off the Florida coast endured only nineteen years before it was washed away. A hurricane that whipped the sea into a frenzy overnight swept the sand from beneath both the tower and keeper's house. Both buildings collapsed, burying the occupants alive. By 1853, the lesson had been learned: the Sandy Key light, for instance, was replaced by a screw pile lighthouse. In 1865 another hurricane roared through the keys, and this time Sand Key disappeared entirely. The screw pile lighthouse still stood, however, and later the island reappeared.

The pile lighthouse thus came into its own along the underwater reefs that break up the seas and prevent the Florida Keys from being totally swept away. The pioneering structure had been built on Carysfort at the northern end of the reefs in 1848. When the first engineers had found that the reef and the sands were too insubstantial for even the screw pile technique, they devised their own pile technique: they drove eight iron piles ten feet down into the seabed up to large, square steel plates that rested on the sea floor so that they resembled nothing so much as giant swords thrust into the sand up to the hilts. Cross members connected each pile and provided a base strong enough for a lighthouse more than 110 feet high.

This and other refinements of the screw pile technique enabled America's lighthouse builders to conquer what was, by 1850, the last part of the North American open coastline to remain unmarked. There are no precise records, but it has been said that in the last fifty years of the nineteenth century there were fewer wrecks between Newfoundland in the north and the Florida Keys in the south than in any *single* year during the last half of the previous century.

First lit in 1852, the Carysfort Reef light (right) was the first of the famous Florida reef pile lights to be built. Its construction took four years and involved driving nine iron piles ten feet into the coral. This well-braced structure has survived storms and hurricanes and continues to warn ships of the shallow reef on which it stands.

In 1748, the British warship *H.M.S. Fowey* was wrecked near the location where this lighthouse (above) was built. Named Fowey Rocks after the ship, it made the old lighthouse at Cape Florida obsolete since the new structure was in a better position to warn ships at sea. Soon to be automated, it is the last manned lighthouse on the Florida reefs.

The light from the fourth order lens of the Georgetown light-station (left) on North Island marks the entrance to Winyah Bay. A plaque above the entrance to the tower reads:

This Light House was Erected
—1811—
Charles Brown Esqr
Superintendent
WALKER & EVANS
Undertakers Charleston S°
Carolina

The lantern of the Cape Romain lighthouse (above right), now gutted and weather-beaten, was last lit in 1947. The framework of the copper-covered lantern dome has been secured with wrought iron tie rods for more than a century. Once the keeper's domain, the forlorn lantern (right) is now a lofty roost for owls and other birds of prey.

The St. Augustine lighthouse (opposite page) was built near the site of an early Spanish observation tower. The brick tower, built in 1874, was later painted with its "barber pole" stripes to make it a better daymark. The Cape Florida light (left) is now a museum piece in the Cape Florida State Park. Eight miles off Key West stands Sand Key and its screw pile lighthouse (bottom). Below: the leaning tower of Cape Romain.

Charleston Light

The Charleston light in South Carolina was witness to the birth of the nation, and to the incident that could have been the death of it – the Civil War. The first lighthouse was built in 1767 on Morris Island at the mouth of the harbour. Its cornerstone bore a plaque reading: "The first stone of this Beacon was laid on the 30th of May 1767 in the seventh year of his Majesty's Reign, George the III." In 1837 this tower replaced by a new lighthouse which stood not far from a relatively new fortification, Fort Sumter, built off the end of what was then known as Lighthouse Island.

There, on April 14, 1861, Union ships began their historic bombardment of the fort, the first act of war between the North and the South. As the ravages of that war continued around Charleston, the lighthouse was severely damaged. Later, it was restored as a first order light, but in 1962, was replaced by the New Charleston Light Station on Sullivans Island and today no longer functions as a lighthouse.

Built on a foundation of piles driven fifty feet deep and a concrete base eight feet thick, the Charleston light (above) withstood a hurricane in 1885 and an earthquake the following year. The surrounding buildings did not fare so well. Erosion and earthquakes have destroyed them all, until only the tower remains standing a quarter of a mile offshore. The new Charleston light was built north of the harbour in 1962.

Opposite page: The Hunting Island light, completed in 1875, stood for less than twenty-five years before it had to be moved to protect it from the sea which was eroding the north end of the island. The cast iron sections were dismantled and re-erected to the south, where it now stands as part of a state park. The anchoring bolts (top left), stairway (top right) and lantern gallery (right) remain.

Standing alone for most of the 106 years since it was built, the Cape Kennedy lighthouse (opposite page) still looks contemporary beside its space age neighbours. The exterior and interior stairways (below) have a nautical flavour with the portholes and davit. Wildlife is still abundant in the region, although not so much so as in bygone days when, it is said, lighthouse keepers used to kill rattlesnakes for oil to lubricate the lens mechanism.

Cape Kennedy Light

In the 1840's the U.S. lighthouse service, still being run by the Treasury, reached the height of inefficiency, and Cape Kennedy Light was proof of the fact. Few real experts in navigation were involved in lighthouse building, and Washington relied heavily on local builders and "connections" to decide navigational needs. Thus, in the 1840's, the sixty-foot-high tower at Cape Kennedy (then known as Cape Canaveral) was built to warn ships of shoals that ran out from the coast. It was, however, too late, and its Winslow Lewis reflector light too dim. From the moment it was lit, mariners complained the light was

a threat rather than an aid to safe passage. Ships had to come in so close to see it they actually placed themselves in danger of coming to grief on the very shoals the light was supposed to help them avoid. When, in the 1850's, the Lighthouse Board was formed, it decided a new 150-foot-high tower should be built. Work did not actually begin, however, until shortly before the Civil War, which halted all lighthouse construction. The first order light was therefore not in service until 1868. Suddenly erosion accelerated, and by 1883 only 192 feet of beach separated the brick-lined cast-iron tower from the open Atlantic. It was disassembled and rebuilt one-and-a-quarter miles inland in 1894.

Tybee Island Light

Tybee Island light at the mouth of the Savannah River in Georgia was the first great navigational aid in the old South. The first ninety-foot-high wooden tower was built in the 1730's as a day mark, but blew down in 1741. It was replaced in 1742 by a tower that displayed a light which would qualify it as the third lighthouse to be built in the country. But the Tybee Island area is best known in history because of the lost love of Florence Martus, renowned earlier this century as the Waving Girl of Elba Island. Florence was the sister of the keeper of the Elba Island light, a few miles inshore from Tybee, the main light for the area. In 1887, Florence was wooed by a young naval lieutenant whose ship was in Savannah Harbour. When he left he promised to return and marry her. "I'll wait for you always," she said. "When you leave Savannah and your ship sails by our house I'll wave farewell with this great white handkerchief. And then, when your ship comes back, I'll be standing by the cottage waiting waving at you." Weeks became months. The sailor didn't write, and Florence didn't know his address. So she began to wave a greeting to each and every ship that passed. By the time her brother, the keeper, retired in 1931, she had been waving at all vessels for forty-four years, and was world famous.

The octagonal brick tower at Tybee Island, painted black with a white band, was originally 100 feet high. Between 1866 and 1867, it was repaired and heightened to 150 feet. Repeated buffeting by gales and earthquakes have cracked the tower, and once broke the first order lens. But the lighthouse still stands, an important aid to navigation at the mouth of the Savannah River. Opposite: St. Simons light, built in 1872.

St. Simons Light

There seems to be a well-authenticated but not particularly malevolent ghost haunting St. Simons light at the entrance to Brunswick harbour, Georgia. In 1907, Carl Svendsen, his wife, and their dog Jinx moved to the island, then almost deserted but now a cottage and resort area, to tend the light. Mrs. Svendsen grew accustomed to putting dinner on the table when she heard her husband clattering down the tower from the light room. One night she did so, but when the footsteps reached the ground, no husband appeared. The dog, Jinx, barked in alarm, then whimpered in fear. She investigated and found her husband still at the top of the tower. At first he didn't believe her. Then, a few days later, he also heard the phantom footsteps, and through the years they both heard the "ghost" often without being able to find an explanation. The Svendsens remained at the lighthouse for around forty years, during which time they learned to live with the phenomenon, although while he lived the dog Jinx remained terrified and would hide whenever the strange footsteps clattered and echoed around the tower. The light is not permanently manned now, but it is said that the tower still is haunted.

Amelia Island and Ponce de Leon Lights

At the mouth of St. Mary's river, which forms the border between Georgia and Florida, stands Amelia Island – a low, mosquito-laden area of near-swamp on which one of the first lighthouses to be built in Florida was erected. The Lighthouse Board dictated that all the towers should be the traditional tapering stone tower capped with a lightroom – a design almost classically Victorian in its functional severity. But local architecture and climate determined the nature of the keeper's quarters, and at Amelia Island the influence of the Ante Bellum tradition could be seen in the galleried, canopied two-storey home occupied by keepers and their families before the light was automated and the house demolished.

Perhaps the most essential part of any house in the area in the mid 1800's was adequate mosquito screening: the insects flourish in the humid swamplands of that coast and sometimes were as big a hindrance to lighthouse builders working in what were then remote, often desolate areas, as were the hostile Seminole Indians. All three elements – remoteness, the Indians and the mosquitoes–conspired against attempts to build a lighthouse south of Amelia Island at Ponce de Leon Inlet (then called Mosquito Inlet) in 1835. The insects delayed the work; oil for the light failed to arrive because the lighthouse was so isolated; and workmen were driven off by the Seminoles. The tower therefore stood lightless until erosion toppled it a few years later. It was almost fifty years before the Lighthouse Board went back to the inlet to build another tower, and that took three years to finish and cost the life of one man.

The lantern and lens at Amelia Island lighthouse (left) is a fine example of mid-nineteenth-century functional elegance. Right: Now lightless, the 150-foot, red brick tower at Ponce de Leon still serves as a daymark for local fishermen and yachtsmen.

Jupiter Inlet Light

Building lighthouses in Florida was a tougher job than anywhere else in the nation, and the great brick and stone towers that stand wherever the land is firm enough are monuments to the endurance of the men who built them. Typically, the Jupiter Inlet Light, some fifteen miles north of Palm Beach, took four years to build, the construction hampered by the climate, the ubiquitous mosquito, and the angry Seminoles. In time, the Seminole wars ended, but the problems of heat and insects remained to make the job of tending the light an unenviable one. Worse, though, are the hurricanes that sweep through the area making the task of maintaining lighthouse efficiency both hazardous and difficult. In recent years the possibility of storm damage to the light has posed the most alarming threat of all. Many of the older lights in service are still equipped with the magnificent Fresnel lenses imported from France a century ago, which have the value of an "antique," since they cannot be readily replaced. Some twenty years ago, a hurricane smashed the lamp room windows at Jupiter Inlet Light, and then either the storm or flying debris actually smashed the bull's eye lens that is the focal part of the lantern. No replacement part was available, and it seemed the light was doomed until technician James Maher demonstrated his resourcefulness. First, he used cement to glue the shattered shards of the lens back into the original lens configuration. Then he meticulously built a brass framework to bind them together. The lens-in-a-frame was re-inserted into the lamp, and Jupiter Inlet Light was back in business.

The great Fresnel lenses with which most older lighthouses are still equipped are irreplaceable today, and so when one bull's eye lens at Jupiter Inlet was smashed during a storm in the 1950's it seemed the entire apparatus would have to be replaced. Then a technician meticulously collected the shards of glass and glued them together, binding them in place with a brass frame. Re-installed, the original Fresnel lens light is still in use.

Farther north, lighthouses are more readily pictured in a setting of bleak rocks and bad-tempered seas. In the south they bask in tropic paradise, as at Jupiter Inlet where a palm tree stands at the lighthouse door (top left); the stairs are of the stucco-covered rock familiar in equatorial regions (top right), and the banyan tree (above) planted by the first keeper in 1860 grew so fast it now looks older than the lighthouse itself.

Cape Florida Light

History shows that two cultures cannot co-exist on the same land: one always becomes dominant and the other decays. Thus, with the fate of northern tribes as a terrible example, the Seminole Indians rebelled when whites flooded south when Florida became part of the United States in 1821.

Since lighthouses were the most visible symbols of white civilization, it was somehow appropriate that one of the most dramatic incidents in the Seminole uprising took place at one of the first lights built in Florida–the Cape Florida Light on the then lonely tip of Key Biscayne. At 4 P.M. on July 23, 1836, eleven years after the light was first lit, keeper John W. B. Thompson opened the back door of his house and found "a large body of Indians within 20 yards of me." Yelling to his Negro assistant, an old man, to follow, Thompson dashed to the brick light tower and bolted the door on the Indians, though a volley of shots "cut my clothes and hat and perforated the door in many places." He fired back from the lighthouse windows, but the Indians stayed and then began a twenty-four-hour nightmare.

Thompson later told this story: "I kept them from the house until dark. They then poured in a heavy fire at all the windows and lantern; that was the time they set fire to the door and to the window even with the ground. The flames spread fast, being fed with the yellow pine wood. Their balls had perforated the tin tanks of oil, consisting of 225 gallons. My bedding, clothing and in fact everything I had was soaked in oil." He and his assistant moved up to the lamp room, covering the scuttle – the hole in the floor that gave access to the room – to prevent flames reaching them.

"At last the awful moment arrived. The crackling flames burst around me. The savages at the same time began their hellish yells. My poor negro looked at me with tears in his eyes, but he could not speak. We went out of the lantern and down to the edge of the platform, two feet wide. The lantern was now full of flames, the lamps and the glasses bursting and flying in all directions, my clothes on fire, and to move from the place where I was would be instant death from their rifles. My flesh was roasting, and to put an end to horrible suffering I got up and threw the keg of gunpowder down the scuttle. Instantly it exploded and shook the tower from top to bottom. It had not the desired effect of blowing me to eternity, but it threw me down the stairs and all the woodwork near the top of the house; it damped the fire for a moment, but it soon blazed as fierce as ever."

Within minutes the assistant was fatally wounded. Thompson, his clothes burned off his back, decided to commit suicide by jumping to the rocks eighty feet below. Just then the blazing wood inside the brick shell fell to the foot of the tower and the fire cooled. The Indians, probably presuming both men dead, plundered the house and made off in Thompson's sloop. It was by then 2 A.M., ten hours after the attack began. At dawn, as Thompson said: "I was now almost as bad off as before. A burning fever on me, my feet shot to pieces, no clothes to cover me, nothing to eat or drink, a hot sun overhead, a dead man by my side, no friend near or any to expect, and placed between 70 and 80 feet from the earth with no chance of getting down."

But help was at hand. The sloop-of-war *Concord* had been twelve miles away when the gunpowder exploded. The crew heard it, came to investigate, and on the afternoon of July 24 found the naked keeper waving from the top of the lighthouse. It took them until the next day, but eventually they shot a line to him from a musket, and he was able to clamber down.

When built in 1825 on the southern extremity of Key Biscayne, Cape Florida lighthouse was the only structure for miles around. It was still isolated in 1836, and was an obvious target for the band of Seminole Indians who besieged the keeper and his assistant in the tower. The keeper survived, though his assistant was killed and the interior of the tower gutted by fire.

Fowey Rocks Light

The iron pile and screw pile lighthouses were among the last lighthouses to be built on the Altantic coast of America. Those shown on these pages represent the final solution to the problem of protecting shipping from the treacheries of the coastline at the southern tip of Florida. Prior to the development of pile lighthouse technology, lightships had been widely used as offshore hazard markers. But lightships were costly to maintain and lethally vulnerable to storms and hurricanes. The first of them to be replaced with an iron pile lighthouse was the one at Carysfort near the northern extremity of the Florida Keys, and the success of this structure prompted the building of several others before 1900. Their construction marked the end of the era of major lighthouse building between Labrador and the Gulf of Mexico. The eastern approaches to the continent were secure. The spread of civilization from Europe to the New World was complete.

Paradoxically (since they are utilitarian structures), lighthouses are often classic examples of man's creativity. At the Fowey Rocks lighthouse, simple triangular angle irons would have been the logical form of ceiling bracket. Yet the men who built the cast and sheet iron structure in the 1870's chose to use the more elaborate, infinitely more pleasing and yet equally functional brackets seen above.

In geography, it begins at Pointe Amour on the frigid, rock-bound coasts of Labrador and ends near Key West (above) in the steamy heat of fecund, tropical Florida. In time, it began in 1716 with the building of Boston Light and ended in the latter half of the 1800's with the completion of the Florida Keys pile lighthouses similar to the successful structure at Fowey Rocks (opposite page). But, by 1900, the chain of lighthouses down the Atlantic coast of North America was completed. The entire eastern seaboard was as safe for man as man could make it. The improvements since have been technological, and new developments have in large part only been possible because the great lighthouses were already in place.

Epilogue

Lighthouses of the type illustrated here will not be built again. In the past, keeping the lights burning and the fog signal sounding required the patience and commitment of the keeper, his family, and his assistants. Today, the function of many such installations has been usurped by electronic navigational aids, and many others have been automated, left to stand, salt-sprayed and rust-stained with windows permanently shuttered. They appear shabby for want of routine housekeeping, but their essential spirit is still there, for they were built for performance, to save men from the sea, not for beauty and not for propaganda.

As technology continues to advance, most of these light stations will remain, standing somehow magically where land, sea and sky meet. A great many of them will become museums and tourist attractions. Indeed, many are such already, generally in federal, provincial or state parks, and conservation areas set up in the wilderness regions that remain in those lonely places where lighthouses were built.

So long as the good intentions of governments endure, these areas will remain free of the generally unlovely and haphazard urban development that litters many of our seashores and river banks. Such open spaces, left largely in the natural state, do not pollute the oceans as the communities of man do; rather they help cleanse it. And since the oceans are now so spoiled that wise men fear for their health, it may be that the lighthouse towers remaining on lonely vigil will come to be symbols of the fight to save the seas from man – a disturbingly ironic twist of history, since they were first built for the opposite purpose.

Dudley Witney

Bibliography

Adamson, H. C. *Keepers of the Lights*. New York: Greenberg, 1955.

Appleton, Thomas E. *Usque ad Mare*. Ottawa: Canada Ministry of Transport, 1968.

Beaver, Patrick. *A History of Lighthouses*. London: Peter Davies, 1971.

Bush, Edward F. *The Canadian Lighthouse*. Canadian Historic Sites: Occasional Papers in Archaeology & History, No. 9, Ottawa: 1975

The Civil Engineer & Architects Journal, Volume V. London, 1842.

Cyclopedia of Useful Arts. London & New York: George Virtue & Co., 1851.

Davenport, Adams, W. H. *Lighthouses and Lightships*. Edinburgh: T. Nelson and Sons, 1871.

De Gast, Robert. *The Lighthouses of the Chesapeake*. Baltimore: The John Hopkins Press, 1973.

Department of Energy, Mines and Resources. *St. Lawrence River Pilot*. First edition. Ottawa: 1966.

Department of Energy, Mines and Resources. *Gulf of St. Lawrence Pilot*. Sixth edition. Ottawa: 1968.

Department of the Environment. *Sailing Directions Nova Scotia (S.E. Coast) and Bay of Fundy*. Fifth Edition. Ottawa: 1972

Department of Marine and Fisheries. *Rules and Instructions for the Guidance of Lightkeepers*. Ottawa: Government Printing Bureau, 1912.

The Edinburgh Encyclopaedia. Vol. 13. Edinburgh: W. Blackwood & S. Waugh, 1830.

Findlay, A. J. *A Description of Lighthouses of the World*. 1867.

Holland, F. Ross, Jr. *America's Lighthouses*. Brattleboro, Vt.: Stephen Greene Press, 1972.

Johnson, Arnold B. *The Modern Lighthouse Service*. Washington: U.S. Government Printing Office, 1889.

Ministry of Transport. *List of Lights, Buoys and Fog Signals NEWFOUNDLAND*. Ottawa: 1975.

Ministry of Transport. *List of Lights, Buoys and Fog Signals ATLANTIC COAST*. Ottawa: 1975.

Newfoundland House of Assembly. *Journals*.

Oke, Robert. "Plans of the Several Light Houses in the Colony of Newfoundland." Unpublished manuscript.

Pratt, Wm. A. *The New American Coast Pilot*. Hartford, Conn.: Hutchinson, 1893.

Putnam, George R. *Sentinel of the Coasts. The Log of a Lighthouse Engineer*. New York: Morton & Co., 1937.

Reynaud, M. Leonce. *Memoirs Upon the Illumination in Beaconage of the Coast of France*. Washington: U.S. Government Printing Office, 1876.

Richardson, E. *We Keep a Light*. Toronto: Ryerson Press, 1945.

Singer, Charles, Holmyard, E. J. and Hall, A. R. *History of Technology Volume II*. New York & London: Oxford University Press, 1954.

Snow, Edward Rowe. *Famous Lighthouses of America*. New York: Dodd, Mead, 1955.

Snow, Edward Rowe. *The Lighthouses of New England 1716-1973*. New York: Dodd, Mead, 1973.

Stephens, David E. *Lighthouses of Nova Scotia*. Windsor, N.S.: Lancelot Press, 1973.

Sterling, Robert T. *Lighthouses of the Maine Coast*. Brattleboro, Vt.: Stephen Daye Press, 1935.

Stevenson, Alan. *A Rudimentary Treatise on the History, Construction, and Illumination of Lighthouses*. London: John Weale, 1850.

Stevenson, D. Alan. *The World's Lighthouses Before 1820*. London: Oxford University Press, 1959.

Strobridge, Truman R. *Chronology of Aids to Navigation and the Old Lighthouse Service*. Washington: United States Coast Guard, 1974.

Talbot, Frederick A. *Lightships and Lighthouses*. London: William Heinemann, 1913.

Texaco Cruising Charts Numbers 1-4. New York: Texaco Waterways Service, 1973.

United States Coast Guard, Department of Transport. *Light List Vol. I Atlantic Coast of the United States CG 158; Vol. II Atlantic and Gulf Coast CG 160*. Washington: U.S. Government Printing Office, 1975.

United States Coast Guard. *Historically Famous Lighthouses*. Washington: U.S.G.P.O., 1957.

United States Department of Commerce. *United States Coast Pilot Atlantic Coast East to Cape Cod*. Washington, 1972.

United States Light-House Establishment. *Instructions to Light Keepers and Masters of Light-House Vessels*. Washington: Government Printing Office, 1902.

Light List

This index includes all the lighthouses described and pictured in this book. Page numbers in bold face refer to illustrations.

Acknowledgements

I wish to express my appreciation to the Ministry of Transport in Canada and the United States Coast Guard, whose co-operation have made this book possible.

Special thanks are due to Thomas E. Appleton, marine historian with Canada's Ministry of Transport, who gave guidance and advice always with cordiality. At the United States Coast Guard in Washington, D.C., Truman Strobridge, historian, and Betty Segedi, picture editor, generously made available much archival material and information.

In their respective areas, the following persons of the Ministry of Transport provided assistance with transportation and local knowledge: W. G. George and Capt. Desmond Leitch, St. John's, Nfld.; Capt. G. J. M. Williams and Louis Hatt, Dartmouth, N.S.; Capt. R. D. Sheils and Capt. H. Caines, Saint John, N.B.; Fred Osborne and Hillard McClennan, Charlottetown, P.E.I.; Lucien Cardinal and Ronaldo Boulanger, Quebec City; and J. K. Rose and H. A. Smith, Prescott, Ontario.

Among the officials of the United States Coast Guard who were always helpful, I would like to mention the following: C.P.O. Chuck Moore, First District, Boston, Mass.; Lt. J. G. Taylor, Fifth District, Portsmouth, Va.; and C.P.O. Jim Gillman, Seventh District, Miami, Florida. I am particularly grateful to C.W.O. Jim Stephens, Third District, Governors Island, N.Y., who willingly gave of his own time and endured my many requests with patience and good humour.

Edward F. Bush of the National Historic Sites, Parks Branch, was always enthusiastic and conscientious in giving information and provided me with much material resulting from his prodigious research in the archives at Ottawa.

For assistance in the preparation of the text special thanks are due to Michael Jacot and Alan Edmonds.

I was also fortunate in having the talents of Paul Newberry for photographic printing and Jack McMaster for rendering of the charts.

The Douglas Library, Queens University, Kingston, and the Gavin Library, Knox College, Toronto, made valuable documents available to me. Also helpful with research material were the Toronto Public Library and the Unionville Centennial Library.

Many lighthouse keepers, fishermen, pilots and friends made my journey more enjoyable and rewarding. I shall especially remember the following: Mr. and Mrs. A. Abbott, Mr. and Mrs. Frank Allen, Roger Balm, Mr. and Mrs. Charles Beard, Norman Benson, André Boisvert, Neil Bryson, Mr. and Mrs. Abner Budgell, Mr. and Mrs. William Caldwell, Mr. and Mrs. Malcolm Campbell, John Carroll, Frank Cole, Arthur Conway, Nora Dawson, Ted Drover, Bessie Wilson Dubois, Mr. and Mrs. Hugh Dulmage, Maurice Dumas, Mr. and Mrs. Harold Farthing, Mr. and Mrs. David Fleming, Bob Gravino, Joseph Greco, Loise Gross, Mr. and Mrs. Garth Gunter, Mrs. Keith Hamilton, Mr. and Mrs. Stewart Hancock, Rev. Brew Hatcher, Lt. Neil Heiner, George Landry, Grover Loening, John MacDonald, James Maher, Jean-Paul Martin, Stewart McIntyre, R. Morong, Noel Myrick, Mr. and Mrs. Louis J. Oglesby, Jr., M. Georges Ozon, Dr. Keith Palmer, Robert Pendleton, Christine Porto, Douglas Rice, William Roberts, Norman Rogers, Andrew and Mayetta St. John, Mr. and Mrs. Harold Sharp, Dr. and Mrs. John Shepperd, Ralph Stone, Dr. and Mrs. Evan Turner, David Walker, Mr. and Mrs. David Walmark, Kadie Walmark, Mr. and Mrs. Walter White and Mr. and Mrs. Bill Williamson.

Dudley Witney

Photo Credits

All photographs and drawings by Dudley Witney except those from the following sources:

Bewick, Thomas, 43

Cyclopedia of Useful Arts, 1851 (engravings), 22, 23 (left), 23 (top right), 30, 38 (left)

A Description of Lighthouses of the World, 1867, A. J. Findlay, 19 (top right)

Edinburgh Encyclopaedia (engravings), 15, 32, 36, 37

The Engineer, March 29, 1889, 19 (upper left)

Lighthouses and Lightships, 1871, W. H. Davenport Adams (engravings), 13, 14, 17

Memoirs Upon the Illumination in Beaconage of the Coast of France, M. Leonce Reynaud, Government Printing Office, Washington, 19 (bottom), 33

Ministry of Transport, Canada, 51 (top left), 65 (bottom), 96 (top), 99 (centre), 102 (left), 103, 110, 111, 112 (top), 118 (top right), 119 (top), 123, 137, 138 (top), 139 (top), 141 (top), 146

Public Archives of Canada, 23 (bottom right), 42, 54, 81 (top), 82 (bottom), 84 (bottom), 100, 101

Royal Ontario Museum, Toronto, 88-89

A Rudimentary Treatise on the History, Construction and Illumination of Lighthouses, 1850, Alan Stevenson, 18, 20 (top left)

United States Coast Guard Archives, 210 (top), 211

United States Coast Guard Photo, 27, 38 (right), 40 (left), 44, 45, 48, 49, 52-53, 178, 179, 191, 193, 196, 208, 209 (right), 210 (bottom), 224

Wonders of Land and Sea, Part X, January 28, 1914, Cassell and Company, Limited, London, 26

The Lighthouse

Typesetting:
Cooper & Beatty Limited, Toronto (text)
Techni-Process Lettering Limited, Toronto (display)

Colour separations and film:
Herzig-Somerville Limited, Toronto

Printing:
Rolph-Clark-Stone Limited, Bramalea

Binding:
John Deyell Company, Lindsay

Design:
David Shaw/McClelland & Stewart Limited

First edition, 1975